CHARACTER TOUR

Character Tour
© 2004 Edwin B. Young

Published by Serendipity House Publishers
Nashville, Tennessee

In cooperation with Fellowship Church Resources
Dallas, Texas

ISBN: 1-5749-4147-X

Dewey Decimal Classification: 155.2
Subject Headings:
CHARACTER \ CHRISTIAN LIFE \ PERSONALITY

1-800-525-9563
www.SerendipityHouse.com

www.fellowshipchurch.com

Printed in the United States of America
10 09 08 07 06 05 04   1 2 3 4 5 6 7 8 9 10

Contents

How To Use This Book

Small groups are a vital part of how we do ministry at Fellowship Church just as they are in many churches around the world. There are a number of different theories on how small groups should work, and they are all great in different ways. The book you are holding is written with our model in mind. So take a minute to read the following explanation, then feel free to adapt as necessary.

Each of our small groups practices a three-part agenda in every meeting. That agenda includes a social time, a discussion time, and a prayer time. Each of these elements share equal importance, but not necessarily equal time. To help you get the most out of this book, we have included an explanation of each of the parts.

The first element of every small-group meeting should be a time of socializing. This phase of the meeting should be about 30% of your time together. Welcome everyone as they arrive at the host home; make visitors feel welcome by introducing yourself and showing genuine interest in them. Enjoy some snacks, or if your group prefers, a meal together. Then move on to the second part of the meeting—the lesson.

The lesson itself may take as much as 50% of your group's meeting time. You may want to start this phase with a short "icebreaker" to get everyone talking. The questions in the "Start It Up" section of each session are what we refer to as "level the playing field" questions that everyone can participate in, regardless of their level of spiritual maturity or Bible knowledge. As your group moves through the "Talk It Up" section in each meeting, remember that it is more important to finish on time than to finish each question. It is okay to skip some questions to allow enough time to take care of the third phase of the small-group time: "Lift It Up."

The "Lift It Up" section is a vital part of every small-group meeting and should take about 20% of your time. You will be able to share with the group what God is doing in your life as well as asking the group to support you in specific prayers. To help focus this time, there are one or two questions that will prompt prayers based on the material you just covered. There is also a space for you to write down your prayer requests so you don't forget them and so you can communicate them clearly when it is your turn. Below that is a place to write down the prayer requests of the people in your group so you can remember to pray for each request throughout the week.

As an additional tool to assist you in your spiritual development journey, 10 devotionals lead up to each of the Sessions 2 through 6. Ten devotionals are provided to accommodate groups that meet every other week, giving material for five days each week during that two-week interval. These will help you develop a daily quiet time with God. To get the absolute most from this book, I challenge you to take 5 or 10 minutes a day to read and apply these devotionals in your life.

God's best!
Ed

Character Tour

Whenever a longtime friend of mine sees somebody do something interesting or a little funny, he gives that person a friendly pat on the back and says in his slow Southern drawl, "You character!" It's a distinctive phrase that I automatically connect with him. It's like hearing, "Here's Johnny!" and instinctively thinking of Ed McMahon on the old "Tonight" show.

I have come to realize over the years, as I have taken some time to reflect on his statement, that every time my friend says those two little words to someone, he is right—we are all characters. That is to say, we are all made up of character.

But what exactly is character? To boil it down to just a few words, character is an outward reflection of our inward connection. We are going to discover through this study that true character is not just what we allow people to see. It's not just something that we put on for show-and-tell; it's an internal thing. Character qualities define who we are from the inside-out.

Sadly, though, in today's world of corporate scandals, flip-flop politics, and morally bankrupt media, true and meaningful character has become an endangered species. Too many of us have allowed ever-changing cultural values to define who we are. We bail out instead of blasting through. We sit down instead of standing up. We get bogged down in the past instead of visualizing the future. We settle for the mundane instead of implementing creativity. And we demonstrate hate instead of sharing God's love.

So, how do we grab hold of the kind of Christ-like character that God wants us to have? How do we develop those uncompromising character qualities in our lives? That's what this study is all about. Over the next several weeks, we are going to take a tour through the Bible and look at some great characters who demonstrated great character. As we book a trip with God's travel agent and embark on this one-of-a-kind Character Tour, my prayer is that, at the end of the journey, we'll be able to hear God say, "You character!"

Which Way is Your Character Morphing?

2 Corinthians 3:18; 1 Peter 1:6-7; Psalm 119:67-71; James 1:2-4

One of the constant realities in today's high-speed world is that things always change. It seems like the rate of change is faster this decade than in the last. Most of us would agree that while some changes in society are positive, convenient, and even promising, many changes are very disturbing.

If we're honest with ourselves, we have to admit that we get pulled down by our humanity and by the society we call home. We are all tainted. Most people no longer believe in absolute truth or objective, universal standards for morality. Fatigue of standing against this tide of moral relativism affects us all. It's as if we are walking up the down escalator and someone keeps cranking up the speed controls. We might even begin to ask, "What's wrong with the idea that I make my own judgments based on how I feel about it?" How do we stay committed in our quest to reflect the absolute and uncompromising image of a holy God?

The answer is character. Character is the outward reflection of our inward connection. In this study we are going to take a Character Tour. As we survey a number of characters in Scripture, we'll see what their character is made of and what their character grows out of.

Start It Up

Do you ever ask the question, "How much am I being changed by my culture?" Are you learning to tolerate what used to repulse you? As you draw close enough to see your reflection in the eye of an unchanging God, do you sometimes see someone you don't really recognize?

1. What is one area of our society where you have seen moral standards slipping? Give an example.

2. What are some practical ways to be a positive moral influence to the world around you?

Talk It Up

Our Character Tour will take us to some of the greatest stops in Scripture.

The first stop is *endurance*. We will check out a man named Noah, who had incredible staying power. He started a project that took him 120 years to complete. We will learn that endurance is stampeding right through the stopping points of life.

From there we will travel to *courage*. The life of Joshua and Caleb will show us how to draw a line in the sand and stand against peer pressure as we hold fast to what we believe.

Then it is on to *love*. God's man, Hosea, followed his Heavenly Father's voice and married a prostitute, and then powerfully demonstrated the beginning point of great character: love in the grip of God's grace.

We will continue to travel on to *creativity*. We won't have to look far in the Bible to find creativity. God The Father invented it, Jesus the Son modeled it, and God the Holy Spirit empowered it.

Finally our Character Tour will stop at *discipline*. Discipline is a foundational character quality, common to those who accomplish much. We will see how God used Daniel in amazing ways because of his commitment.

Before our tour begins, let's investigate three fascinating Bible passages that disclose what character is all about.

Character Developed Through Metamorphosis

Read 2 Corinthians 3:18

Paul refers to the Old Testament story of Moses to explain that since Jesus came and brought new life into the world, we have full access to God because His Spirit now lives in us. In Old Testament times, God used more of an outside-in approach to develop faith in His people. That has changed.

When referring to Christ-followers, Paul uses the word "transformed," from which we get the word "metamorphosis." It means to change from the "inside-out." It is a continuous morphing experience. It is not dependent upon anything on the outside. That is why we define character as "the outward reflection of our inward connection."

Now, the obvious question: who or what should we be connected to? **The simple answer: Jesus.** He revolutionized the character development process through His work on the cross. He is the essence of perfectly developed character. When we allow Him to dwell in us as Master, instead of visiting Him on the mountain or in the tent of meeting (as Moses did), He literally begins a character exchange within us. He delivers the promise and possibility of new character all at once, and then through our daily obedience He begins the eternal character exchange piece by piece. So, we are in the process of being transformed into "ever-increasing glory."

3. What are some ways you can stay connected to Jesus day in and day out?

session one

Character Forged in the Fires of Trials and Testing

Read 1 Peter 1:6-7

Two of the most useful tools in the hand of God used throughout history to reveal and develop our character are trials and testing. Peter, who wrote these verses, knew a lot about trials and testing. He knew a lot about messing up, too. Peter was part of Jesus' inner circle, and yet he denied and failed Jesus during the time of His arrest, trial, and death on the cross. Later, after His return from the grave, Jesus lovingly restored Peter and set him on a path toward deeper character transformation.

You see, God is more interested in our growth than our success. He knows we need times of failure and suffering to test what is within us and motivate us to follow Him in the transformation process.

Look at the phrase in 1 Peter 1:7: "so that your faith—of greater worth than gold, which perishes even though refined by fire—may be proved genuine." Peter paints a powerful image of a goldsmith purifying gold. He cranks up the heat and the increased temperature causes the impurities to rise to the top. Then he scrapes the impurities off and tosses them aside. He repeats this same process again and again. The goldsmith knows the gold is ready—that it is purified—when he can clearly see his reflection in it.

There are times when we may feel that God is asleep at the switch. We fear that the temperature is too hot and the time has run away. Just when we feel like we can't take it any more, He sees His reflection in our lives. That is how He builds deep, lasting, mature, one-of-a-kind character in His children. This passage reveals the value God places on transformation. He allows "heat" to come in various forms so that we realize who we are on the inside and earnestly desire inner character exchange.

4. How has God used times of testing in your life to reveal a deeper need for Him?

5. What are the consequences of refusing to stay in the heat long enough to allow our impurities to rise to the top?

Character Deepened by Afflictions and Suffering

Read Psalm 119:67-71

This short passage powerfully and clearly illustrates that struggles and correction come into our lives to bring certain and permanent change to our character and ultimately our actions. The word "afflicted" can be accurately translated "humbled." The phrase, "I went astray" refers not to accidental or innocent mistakes, but to really blowing it. It means that out of stubbornness and willfulness, we decide to do life our own way. This is a dangerous inclination for all of us. If this does not come out of us, it will ruin us. So what is a loving God to do? So often He uses our affliction and suffering to generate a deeper work of transformation. David seems to indicate that the only real casualty in metamorphosis is our pride.

6. Why do you think God uses suffering to reveal flaws and motivate character transformation?

7. What are the internal and external roadblocks that keep you from experiencing this transformation?

session one

SMALL-GROUP SESSION

Lift It Up

Read James 1:2-4

God wants us to do more than just survive the struggles of life. He wants us to experience joy in spite of the pain, because we know that He is transforming our character through the tough times.

8. When it comes to developing Christ-like character, what are the easy things we can do to help each other continue to grow? What are the hard things?

Take time to pray specifically for each other in those areas where you sense God is leading you to develop more Christ-like character.

My Prayer Needs:

_____

_____

_____

_____

My Group's Prayer Needs:

_____

_____

_____

_____

_____

_____

_____

_____

DEVOTIONALS

Noble Character

Day 1

Now the Bereans were of more noble character than the Thessalonians, for they received the message with great eagerness and examined the Scriptures every day to see if what Paul said was true. (Acts 17:11)

The description of noble character could not be any more clear than what is presented in this passage. It is almost as if someone specifically asked Paul, "what does noble character look like?"

What a great combination of openness and self-responsibility is found in this verse! It is clear that the Bereans were not "baby birds" willing to swallow anything and everything without examination. But the amazing thing is that they weren't mean-spirited about it either.

We too can maintain an open, gracious posture without being gullible. A mature person with deep character is able to make room for the teaching of others and still remain in charge of his own spiritual growth.

Is your character noble like that of the Bereans? What can you do to either improve your eagerness to learn from others or take more responsibility for your own spiritual development?

_____

_____

_____

_____

_____

_____

DEVOTIONALS

Perseverance, Character, and Hope

Day 2

We also rejoice in our sufferings, because we know that suffering produces perseverance; perseverance, character; and character, hope. And hope does not disappoint us, because God has poured out his love into our hearts by the Holy Spirit, whom he has given us. (Romans 5:3-5)

It is often said that great character is formed during times of suffering and trials. But it is also said, and I believe more accurately, that suffering and trials reveal the character that is present in a person. These two truths are really flip sides on the same coin.

Despite the difficulties of life, it is good character that leads us into a place of hope and promise. Life can disappoint us, but the hope that we have because of God's love does not and cannot disappoint. Notice, however, that this character is the result of perseverance, so it does not come without commitment and sacrifice.

Can you honestly say that you rejoice in times of suffering and trials? Ask God today to give you a fresh outlook on the suffering you may be experiencing. What is God revealing to you about how He wants to grow your character?

DEVOTIONALS

Deep Roots

Day 3

Blessed is the man who does not walk in the counsel of the wicked or stand in the way of sinners or sit in the seat of mockers. But his delight is in the law of the LORD, and on his law he meditates day and night. He is like a tree planted by streams of water, which yields its fruit in season and whose leaf does not wither. Whatever he does prospers. (Psalm 1:1-3)

Standing tall against the elements, like the tree in verse three, will only happen when your roots are deep. Roots take time to develop. See your time with God today as a strength deposit toward a challenging trial you will experience in the future.

Drinking deeply from God's source of life and truth in the Bible will not only produce in you what you need at the right time, but it will also give you great happiness in your journey.

Ask God today to talk with you about your roots. Where do they need to go deeper? What can you do to soak your roots more thoroughly with the water of Scripture?

_____
_____
_____
_____
_____
_____
_____
_____
_____

DEVOTIONALS

Good Calls

Day 4

Let the peace of Christ rule in your hearts, since as members of one body you were called to peace. And be thankful. Let the word of Christ dwell in you richly as you teach and admonish one another with all wisdom, and as you sing psalms, hymns, and spiritual songs with gratitude in your hearts to God. (Colossians 3:15-16)

The phrase "rule in your hearts" is lifted out of the world of first century athletics and paints the picture of an umpire presiding over an athletic competition.

A person of excellent character has a constant awareness that even in the heat of competition there must be a voice of reason and sound judgment. For the game to go well, we must acknowledge the umpire's authority.

Passive people, those sitting on the sidelines, have less need of an umpire than those fully engaged in the real "game" of life. Stay in the game and acknowledge the place of the "Umpire" in your heart today. Submit to His "calls" and experience His peace.

How are you doing? Does you heart feel peaceful? Is there an area of your life where you are not submitting to God's "calls"?

_____

_____

_____

_____

_____

_____

_____

DEVOTIONALS

You—God's Masterpiece

Day 5

For we are God's workmanship, created in Christ Jesus to do good works, which God prepared in advance for us to do. (Ephesians 2:10)

Notice that this verse does not say that we "were" God's workmanship; it is an ongoing process. God is a master craftsman with a tireless determination to make us into that picture of us that He holds in His mind. A master craftsman works to please his own eye and will not cut corners or stop until the work is complete—perfect.

Can you imagine God standing over you today with tools in hand, anxious to continue His masterpiece? You are a vital part of God's portfolio. Gladly welcome His master touch in your life today.

Do you see yourself as a masterpiece? What do you think God created you for? What special work has He prepared just for you?

_____

_____

_____

_____

_____

_____

_____

_____

_____

_____

DEVOTIONALS

God's Handrails

Day 6

If the LORD delights in a man's way, he makes his steps firm; though he stumble, he will not fall, for the LORD upholds him with his hand. (Psalm 37:23-24)

Divine favor, which occurs as God is pleased with our choices, becomes the handrails that keep us on course as we continue our journey. It is as if God says to us, "When you are walking in my ways, I will hold you up."

This is the picture of a God who is patient with our humanity. Knowing we will stumble along the way, He promises to steady us and pick us up when necessary.

Put your trust in God's ability to stabilize you today. Your job is to continue to travel the path He wants you to take. His job is to make sure you get there.

Do you think that the Lord is "delighting in your way"? If you are stumbling on your path in life, what can you do to learn to lean on His hands?

_____

_____

_____

_____

_____

_____

_____

17

DEVOTIONALS

Got You Covered

Day 7

Though I walk in the midst of trouble, you preserve my life; you stretch out your hand against the anger of my foes, with your right hand you save me. The LORD will fulfill [his purpose] for me; your love, O LORD, endures forever—do not abandon the works of your hands. (Psalm 138:7-8)

Do you ever feel like "trouble" is a stray dog that follows you wherever you go? There is comfort in knowing that even when problems are nipping at your heels, God is there to watch your back.

God has put himself on the line to reveal and fulfill His purpose in your life. No matter how hard you try, you can't do life successfully under your own power. But, with His help, you can make it through any situation and live out His plan for you.

Because His love endures forever, He is going to stick with you for the long haul. Allow the love of God to fill you right now. Release your life into God's hands, and watch the fear of not measuring up flee from you.

How comfortable are you with releasing your life into God's hands? Can you trust Him to fulfill His purpose in you even in the midst of trouble?

_____

_____

_____

_____

_____

DEVOTIONALS

Turn on the Lights

Day 8

The path of the righteous is like the first gleam of dawn, shining ever brighter till the full light of day. But the way of the wicked is like deep darkness; they do not know what makes them stumble.
(Proverbs 4:18-19)

Pretty much anything we try to do in the dark is much more difficult, takes more time, and is more dangerous than if we could do it in the light.

The enemy of our souls, Satan, loves to see us scurry up the path in the relative darkness, doing "good" things but not really being connected with God. We so easily fall into the trap of thinking that all God wants is for us to just do the right thing, when He really wants our hearts to yearn for His presence and grow in the process.

As you begin to walk in the right way, according to God's will, His light will become increasingly brighter in your life and you will see your way more clearly. Take the first step now. If you have any unconfessed sin against God or others, confess it today. Then begin to move forward, quickly and safely in His ever increasing light.

How bright is the light on your path? What areas of sin do you need to confess and yield to the Lord so that you can experience more and more of His light in your life?

_____

_____

_____

_____

_____

Before Session Two

DEVOTIONALS

Faith that Doesn't Fail

Day 9

"Simon, Simon, Satan has asked to sift you as wheat. But I have prayed for you, Simon, that your faith may not fail. And when you have turned back, strengthen your brothers." (Luke 22:31-32)

It is not hard to imagine that when Jesus said, "I have prayed for you," there was real power in that. Heaven stood ready to respond.

Yet, Jesus' words reveal an interesting life philosophy. It is as if He was saying to Peter, "I know you are going to stumble and fall; my main concern is that you hold on to your faith and get back up." He has the same message for you today.

How encouraging it is for us fellow travelers to realize that Jesus has a realistic picture of our ability to really mess up. Because of His love, He desires to outfit us with a faith rugged enough to be brushed off and put back to work.

Thank God today that He has sustained you through all of your tumbles in the dirt and thank Him in advance for the times ahead when He'll be there to pull you up again. Turn back to Him for forgiveness and a fresh start.

How comfortable are you with having failures in your life? How do you need to adjust your thinking either about being too complacent with your failures or about beating yourself up for your past?

_____

_____

_____

20

DEVOTIONALS

Fruit Branches

Day 10

Remain in me, and I will remain in you. No branch can bear fruit by itself; it must remain in the vine. Neither can you bear fruit unless you remain in me. "I am the vine; you are the branches. If a man remains in me and I in him, he will bear much fruit; apart from me you can do nothing. (John 15:4-5)

One the most difficult things in the Christian faith is to "remain" anywhere while traveling 100 miles an hour through life. We seem to be better at "doing" than we are at remaining or "being." As we rush around disconnected from God, we wonder why we have so little fruit to show.

Can you remember a time when you felt more connected to God? A time when you set aside more time to just "be" in His presence—to listen, learn and respond? If you can, go back to that time and connect with Him again. If this is a foreign concept to you, get away for a short time and try it.

Fruit grows naturally when it is connected to the source of nutrition. Ask God to give you the humility to admit your lack of connection. Then, just as the branch does with the vine, get connected and hang out!

What is your comfort level with putting more focus on remaining in relationship with God, and less on doing things for God? How can you begin to make that transition?

_____

_____

_____

_____

_____

Will Your Endurance Hold Out?

Genesis 6:8-21; Hebrews 11:1; 12:1-3

Looking back over the course of your life, are there things you regret having quit? Maybe it was an educational or business opportunity. Maybe you quit on a friend, or a spouse, or a child. Maybe you feel like you gave up on God. Scroll back through your life and just think about those times that you stopped ... gave up. Feelings of regret or even remorse follow times like these.

As I look back over my life, I can think of many situations when I have felt that regret and remorse. One happened when I was about 16 years of age. I had been asking my parents for a car and they struck a deal with me. They asked me to first read a biography of Sam Houston. So, I began to read it, but I never finished. What I didn't realize was that just a few pages from the end, my parents had written a note rewarding me with my first car. But because I didn't finish the book, I never saw the note and had to go the whole long summer without my new set of wheels.

Start It Up

All of us can relate in some way to the experience of getting tired, discouraged, or just plain bored, and not finished something that we started. It might be something that we felt very passionate about at one time. We may even have put forth a lot of effort or expense, but still we didn't see it through.

session two

1. Looking at the world around you, what areas do you feel are most often affected by a lack of endurance? Why did you choose those areas?
   a. Personal fitness/health
   b. Marriage happiness
   c. Parenting effectiveness
   d. Career goals
   e. Financial plans
   f. Hobby development
   g. Life goals
   h. Reaching out to others/ministry
   i. Other _____

2. Look back over your life and share an example where you wish you would have shown more endurance. What could have happened if you had seen the situation through?

Talk It Up

It seems that we live in a society that almost applauds quitting. Our culture seems to have geared itself up to expect people not to follow through. Many people would rather bail out than blast through, leave than last, throw in the towel than stay in the game. We want month-to-month apartment leases, escape clauses in contracts, prenuptial agreements in marriage, and free agency in pro sports. A lot of people have job-quitting, vow-forgetting, excuse-making, and work-faking mentalities that flee from the Character Tour destination of endurance.

So What is Endurance?

Endurance is definitely on the endangered character quality list, but what is it really, and how do we develop it? Endurance is stampeding through those stopping points of life. It's painstakingly whacking down the walls that block us from achievements. It is a quality that we desperately need, but we certainly don't see much in our day.

With our lack of models today, let's look at the life of a guy from the Bible who really modeled endurance. His endurance is so well known that you could say he is the "poster child" for endurance. Our endearing endurer is none other than Noah, the guy who built the really big boat right in the middle of the desert without a cloud in the sky.

God's Grace and Favor Help Us Endure

Read Genesis 6:1-9

The world had degenerated to such a degree that God was sorry He made mankind and wanted to wipe out the face of the earth. Yet, verse eight says that Noah "found favor" with God. This is one of the first and clearest references to the grace of God in the Bible. The phrase "found favor" is a Hebrew term referring to a superior person giving undeserved favor to an inferior person. In the passage there is almost a sudden, unexpected quality to this experience. "Found" doesn't signify the idea of having something because of petition or demand. Rather, it implies more of a surprise, though not necessarily without some cause.

In verse nine we see a possible cause to this effect of God's favor. It says that "Noah was a righteous man, blameless among (or as compared to) the people of his time, and he walked with God."

3. Describe a time when you have been surprised by "finding undeserved favor" with someone. Why did it surprise you?

4. How do you imagine Noah "walked with God" on a daily basis? What might this "walk" look like today?

Faith is Foundational to Enduring

Read Genesis 6:11-21

One of the things bound to happen to us when we walk with God is that He will speak with us, maybe not audibly, but we will clearly know His direction for our lives. Sometimes what He communicates can be confusing or scary. He told Noah, "I want you to build a boat." Now, we have to get a grip on how crazy this must have seemed to Noah because, chances are, Noah had never seen a boat. Why would he? He lived in the desert, he didn't live near a sea, and it had never rained before. Scholars believe that, up to this time, the earth's vegetation was sustained through a heavy dew that settled in each night instead of from rainfall. It is possible that Noah had never even seen a puddle before, let alone a body of water that could sustain a boat the size God was asking him to build.

5. Hebrews 11:1 says that "faith is being sure of what we hope for and certain of what we do not see." What do you think Noah's first reaction to God's request might have been? What kind of faith crises do you think he experienced before and during the construction process?

6. Has God ever asked something of you that seemed totally ridiculous from your perspective or that was so far outside your experience that it made no sense? Tell about it.

If it wasn't enough that the idea of building a boat blew Noah's mind, the size specifications for that boat were massive! God asked him to build a boat 450 feet long, 75 feet wide and 45 feet high. So not only was Noah's faith blown out of the water (water, which he had never seen), but the job was a nightmare, certainly larger than anything he had ever undertaken in his life. On top of mustering the faith to do the job and enduring all of the job difficulties, he also had to convince some people to help him. He had to inspire faith in others as well.

The monumental scope of the job wasn't the only complication. Noah was 500 years old when he was asked to start this project. Then, it took him 120 years to complete it. Now that's endurance by anybody's definition! I don't know about you, but after say 80 or 90 years, I would have been complaining, "God, come on. I've been watching the weather channel. I don't see any clouds. What's the deal? Everybody in the country thinks I've lost my mind!"

The Bible says that when Noah, his family, and all the animals finally walked into the finished ark ... they still had an endurance test ahead. They boarded the ship, God sealed the door, and there they sat high and dry for seven long, hot, smelly, cramped days before the rain began to fall!

7. What are some common reasons people give when they quit something?

8. How can we determine when God wants us to endure in a situation and when He wants us to let something go?

Encouragement From Others and Dumping Hindrances Help Us Endure

It's time to get really practical with this endurance thing. We see that Noah demonstrated great endurance and we may be thinking, "that's great, but how do I do that?"

Read Hebrews 12:1-3

The first thing we need to do is get our heads "in the clouds" with people of faith who now witness our struggles. Those who have gone before us and demonstrated endurance have something to teach us. Think about old Moses saying to us, "stand up and be a leader ... you can do it!" David encourages us to face the giants in our lives, "just a few smooth stones in faith, man" he says. Even Rahab the prostitute chimes in, "I don't care what you have done, God can still use you in an awesome way!"

And that is just a small sampling of the great cloud of witnesses that have gone before us. If we are really in touch with a cheering section like that we can't help but feel encouraged to endure.

9. Who in your life has a story that really gives you that extra boost you need to hang in there when endurance is required? Share the story.

"Let us throw off everything that hinders and the sin that so easily entangles" is a great picture. It is as if a runner is in the long grueling race and then realizes that he is running in combat boots and a floor-length, wool trench coat. He knows he'll never win this way, so he just starts peeling these hindrances off and throwing them to the side.

10. What is one thing that you can throw off today that will help you run with more endurance?

Lift It Up

Let us fix our eyes on Jesus, the author and perfecter of our faith, who for the joy set before him endured the cross, scorning its shame, and sat down at the right hand of God. (Hebrews 12:2)

Connection With God is Critical to Enduring!

The enemy of our souls, Satan, is constantly trying to get us to cross over that subtle line that lies between trying to endure in God's power and trying to endure on our own. Jesus could never have endured all the way to the cross without His intimate, constant connection to the Father. He didn't make it just because He was really good and unbelievably disciplined. He was able to endure because as He said, "I and the Father are one." Not only was Jesus God, but He also had clear connection and constant communication with the Father.

Christ-followers are able to experience that kind of connection to God through the Holy Spirit. We may not hear the Father as well as Jesus did, but we can hear Him much better than we do now. Remember, character is the

session two

SMALL-GROUP SESSION

outward reflection of our inward connection. We aren't perfect, as Jesus was, but we do have the same Spirit He had. Because He finished strong ... so can we!

11. Realizing that endurance and finishing well don't come easily for anyone, please share one of your "running the race" stories with the group. Be sure to highlight how God provided strength and encouragement in your race.

Take time to pray each other into the "ark" of God's safety and deliverance.

My Prayer Needs:

_____

_____

_____

_____

_____

My Group's Prayer Needs:

_____

_____

_____

_____

_____

_____

_____

_____

DEVOTIONALS

Inseparable Love

Day 1

Who will bring any charge against those whom God has chosen? It is God who justifies. Who is he that condemns? Christ Jesus, who died—more than that, who was raised to life—is at the right hand of God and is also interceding for us. Who shall separate us from the love of Christ? Shall trouble or hardship or persecution or famine or nakedness or danger or sword? (Romans 8:33-35)

As we face barriers in our journey it is helpful to remember that Christ has gone before us to prove that our sinful flesh, the world, and even the devil himself cannot stop us unless we allow ourselves to be stopped.

Though nothing can separate us from God's love, some things like fear, worry, unbelief, and quitting can keep us from experiencing it. Don't let those self-imposed barriers keep you from His soul-satisfying love.

How often do you feel separated from the love of Christ, and in what types of situations does this occur? What can you do to rid yourself of, these self-imposed barriers?

_____

_____

_____

_____

_____

_____

_____

_____

_____

DEVOTIONALS

Strength to the End

Day 2

He will keep you strong to the end, so that you will be blameless on the day of our Lord Jesus Christ. God, who has called you into fellowship with his Son Jesus Christ our Lord, is faithful. (1 Corinthians 1:8-9)

Following God for a month, a year, or a decade is good. But the hallmark of a fully devoted follower of Christ is someone who stays with Him for a whole lifetime.

Take note of the striking and central phrase "keep you strong." This phrase carries with it the idea that as you make a life-long commitment to walking with the Lord, it is He that will keep you strong. He doesn't leave us out here to walk this road alone; He gives us the stuff we need, one day at a time.

Much like other relationships, the harder we work at them, the better they get and the more energy they build. Put faithfulness into the bank of life today and God will add to it the strength you need for tomorrow.

Have you settled your commitment to the Lord? Are you in this for the long haul, and how would anyone know this?

_____

_____

_____

_____

_____

_____

DEVOTIONALS

Encouragement to Endure

Day 3

Therefore, my dear brothers, stand firm. Let nothing move you. Always give yourselves fully to the work of the Lord, because you know that your labor in the Lord is not in vain. (1 Corinthians 15:58)

There are few things more empowering for us than to be in relationship with those who know us and cheer for us. People around us are able to provide a perspective that we often lose sight of. The Apostle Paul offered this fresh perspective when he ended his letter to the Corinthians with a huge dose of encouragement to endure.

Sometimes we get so busy that we lose touch with those who can encourage and challenge us to grow in our spiritual lives.

Call today and schedule lunch or coffee with a friend who is willing to walk with you as you grow.

When you think about the people that encourage you most, who comes to mind? What are some ways you can regularly encourage and build each another up?

_____

_____

_____

_____

_____

_____

_____

DEVOTIONALS

Standing Firm

Day 4

Now it is God who makes both us and you stand firm in Christ. He anointed us, set his seal of ownership on us, and put his Spirit in our hearts as a deposit, guaranteeing what is to come. (2 Corinthians 1:21-22)

This is a great verse to remember when you feel like you're going to fall out from the pressure. The Apostle Paul lists three powerful things God has done to guarantee that we can stand.

He has anointed us. This same phrase is used for inaugurating kings, priests, and prophets. Paul uses it here to announce to all of Christ's followers that we have been blessed with all we need. We can stand with regal confidence.

His seal authenticates us. It's like being notarized. The seal proves we are the real deal—we belong to God. Satan, our enemy, must stand in respect.

Inside every Christ-follower is the Holy Spirit, God active and powerful. When the Holy Spirit is working in us, it proves we belong to God. He is the reason we know that we can make it. He is as close as our thoughts.

Thank God today for the complete genius of His plan and provision.

How would your response to pressure change if you didn't have God standing with you? How can you lean on Him more?

_____

_____

_____

_____

_____

DEVOTIONALS

"Do Gooders"

Day 5

Let us not become weary in doing good, for at the proper time we will reap a harvest if we do not give up. Therefore, as we have opportunity, let us do good to all people, especially to those who belong to the family of believers. (Galatians 6:9-10)

Have you noticed that spring always follows winter? No matter how long and cold the winter is ... spring always comes. If we look back over our lives we will see many of our own "winters" that somehow, against all odds, we endured.

But, it can be hard to wait for God's timing. This is especially true when we are walking alongside others who are hurting and waiting.

If you are "becoming weary" as you support others around you, search your heart to be sure that you haven't gotten locked in to a certain timetable that God may not be as committed to.

Allow God to decide when the seeds you have planted should push their way up through the soil of another person's life. As for you ... keep doing good. You never know when the seeds you plant will start to grow.

In what area of your life are you becoming weary in doing good? How can you overcome it?

_____

_____

_____

_____

_____

DEVOTIONALS

A Greater Power

Day 6

"Be strong and courageous. Do not be afraid or discouraged because of the king of Assyria and the vast army with him, for there is a greater power with us than with him. With him is only the arm of flesh, but with us is the LORD our God to help us and to fight our battles." And the people gained confidence from what Hezekiah the king of Judah said. (2 Chronicles 32:7-8)

"Be strong and courageous. Do not be afraid or discouraged." Who doesn't need to hear these words sometimes? Just as the people listening to these words were encouraged, so can we be as we stand before our enemies and the trials of life.

The awesome thing about God speaking through people is that sometimes the very thing we need to hear is a voice like ours saying the truth like God. Often the voice of the Spirit is so very quiet. We do not always have the desire or the discipline to sit still long enough for the volume to increase.

We need to be realigned by truth-telling, compassionate friends so that we might stand against the bluffs and lies of the enemy. We can also be the one who gives strength to the weak legs of a friend intimidated in battle.

What situations in your life are causing you to be fearful or discouraged? How can you get more in tune with God's power and perspective?

_____

_____

_____

_____

DEVOTIONALS

Things Seen and Heard

Day 7

Peter and John replied, "Judge for yourselves whether it is right in God's sight to obey you rather than God. For we cannot help speaking about what we have seen and heard." (Acts 4:19-20)

Peter and John were two of Jesus' disciples. They had just watched Him be executed and then come back to life again. Now they were standing in front of their enemies. This is not a cute religious story with a happy ending. Their defiance was sure to cost them big—likely they would be killed.

What could they possibly gain by continuing to agitate the authorities? Nothing! So why did they? Their contact with Jesus gave them no choice.

The key to their courage was their first-hand experience with the Savior of the World. "Seen and heard," says it all. It wasn't an idea of God or a creed. It was a person that they had lived so closely with for three years.

God did not leave us with a second-hand experience either. When we experience Jesus first-hand, we will have the courage to stand up tall and say it loud!

Truthfully, could you stand up with the courage that Peter and John did? What things need to happen in your life to give you more first-hand encounters with the Lord Jesus?

_____

_____

_____

_____

_____

DEVOTIONALS

Blazing Furnaces

Day 8

Shadrach, Meshach and Abednego replied to the king, "O Nebuchad-nezzar, we do not need to defend ourselves before you in this matter. If we are thrown into the blazing furnace, the God we serve is able to save us from it, and he will rescue us from your hand, O king. But even if he does not, we want you to know, O king, that we will not serve your gods or worship the image of gold you have set up." (Daniel 3:16-18)

It took a lot of courage to face down such a notoriously powerful king. It took great boldness to express unwavering faith in an invisible God. But it was off-the-charts courageous to leave their fate in the hands of a God who might or might not deliver them from a horrible death.

Only a deep belief in the very nature of God can generate such assurance in times of troubling uncertainty. Such release comes to your spirit when you can place your jumbled up life into the hands of a trustworthy God and say, "do what you want with it … it doesn't matter, I'm going to follow you.

Feel the courage well up in your soul when you see God clearly enough to say, "I'll trust you regardless of how my situation comes out."

What are you facing today that requires this kind of blazing faith? How much do you need to see your faith increase so that you can step into the fiery trial that God has set before you?

_____

_____

_____

_____

_____

DEVOTIONALS

God's Gigantic Deliverance

Day 9

"Your servant has killed both the lion and the bear; this uncircumcised Philistine will be like one of them, because he has defied the armies of the living God. The LORD who delivered me from the paw of the lion and the paw of the bear will deliver me from the hand of this Philistine." (1 Samuel 17:36-37)

Just as David could point to times in the past where he was able to overcome odds that seemed impossible, we too have experiences in our past that prepare us for the future.

The problem is that we hold on to our failures better than we do to our past successes. The times when we didn't overcome an obstacle stick to us like lint from the dryer. Those failures cling to us and influence our image of who we are and what we can accomplish.

It takes great discipline and intention to drag with us into our future those times that we did "kill both the lion and the bear." Ask the Holy Spirit today to bring to your mind the times in your life when God helped you to overcome. Let those memories give you courage today.

What have been some of those victories in your life? Are you allowing your mind to linger more on past failures or victories?

_____

_____

_____

_____

_____

DEVOTIONALS

Courage to Die

Day 10

Then Thomas (called Didymus) said to the rest of the disciples, "Let us also go, that we may die with him." (John 11:16)

What had Thomas experienced by this point in his pilgrimage to cause him to want to die with Jesus? What had he seen in the eyes of Jesus that had caused him to love him this much? What touched him so deeply that he cared so little for his own life?

In this answer lies the secret of courage! Experiencing Jesus on a daily basis radically shifts our perception of what is worth holding on to in life. All Thomas knew for sure is that he wasn't going to let go of Jesus, even if it cost him his life.

What a way to live! You can spend the entire day with Jesus today, through the Spirit who lives in you. Ask Him to make Jesus so real that you abandon all other pursuits that could cause you to put Jesus aside.

Has your experience with Jesus been as radical as Thomas's? What will motivate you to know and walk with Jesus more closely?

_____
_____
_____
_____
_____
_____
_____
_____

Is Your Courage Collapsible?

Numbers 13 – 14; Joshua 1:1-9; John 21:15-19

In today's economy, one of the features often sought after with many products is collapsibility. Does is fold up? Does it get smaller? These are important questions on the minds of consumers. High chairs are collapsible. Cell phones are collapsible. Camping equipment is collapsible. Even some cars are now collapsible.

One of the biggest reasons we want things to be collapsible is so we can easily put them away when we're not using them. Convenience is the driving value.

Today we are going to discuss something that appears to be collapsible for convenience, but it should never be: courage. Doing what is right no matter what it costs us—standing tall even if we have to stand alone—is what courage is all about. In fact, we could define courage as a God-given ability to stand.

As we continue our Character Tour, we will see that courage stands as one of the rarest qualities. Character is the outward reflection of our inward connection. This is certainly true of courage. It comes from deep within us. The more unlikely the person or situation, the more stunning and compelling is the act of courage.

Start It Up

Courage is a rare commodity, so any time we see an act of courage, it really stands out.

session three

1. What is the greatest account of courage that you have witnessed lately? (It can be from a book, news story, movie, or real life.)

2. What is the most courageous thing you have ever done? What did you have to overcome to follow through with action?

Talk It Up

Our Character Tour takes us to the edge of the Jordan river where we find the children of Israel, about one million of them, preparing to cross over into the promised land. The chosen people had been miraculously freed from Egyptian slavery. Many mind-blowing signs and wonders had been performed by God: parting the Red Sea, feeding them with manna from heaven, and other amazing feats. So here they are now on the brink of closing the most stunning real estate deal in the history of the world: claiming the promised land! Right before the title exchange, God does something very unusual. He calls a quick time out and instructs Moses to choose a leader from each tribe and send them over to scout out the land. With a detailed list of what to check out and bring back, Moses sent them out on their secret mission. All 12 went out with great courage and searched out the land for 40 days.

session three

Alarming Reports and Wavering Faith

Read Numbers 13:26-33

Things started out so positively. The spies showed the fruit and testified that the land was everything promised and more. So what happened? They just couldn't get off their "buts." They turned from courageous to cowardly on the power of a little three letter word ... "but!" Once they started with the fears and anxieties, they just kept coming. They entered the "moan zone," and the whole situation went from bad to worse as their courage collapsed.

3. Given their incredible history with God, why do you think the Israelites were afraid now?

In Numbers 13:30 we see a glimmer of hope. Not all of the 12 collapsed their courage and put it away. Two of the 12, who saw the same walled cities and put their feet in the same giant footprints, came back with a much different perspective. Numbers says that Caleb silenced the people. That must have been an awesome sight. Undoubtedly he was one who commanded respect. His confident stance and positive words may have held sway over the crowd for a few minutes, but it didn't last. Can't you just hear the murmuring begin to buzz and swell again to a roar, keying off the folded arms and shaking heads of the 10 who stood behind Caleb as he spoke? Courage can set you apart and it can also bring on some very lonely times.

"We seemed like grasshoppers in our own eyes, and we looked the same to them." This is a fascinating statement. The New American Standard version of the Bible translates "we seemed like" as "we became like." This is the testimony of shrinking courage of 10 of the 12 spies. The other two, Joshua and Caleb, while not denying the report of the size of these huge men, didn't draw the same conclusions. They did not feel smaller because they were focused on a big God.

The Feeding Frenzy of Negativism

Read Numbers 14:1-4

The negativity spread like wild fire! The people were afraid and even panicked. It was almost like someone yelled FIRE! This brings a strong reminder that negativity really sells! People buy it! It seems like negative attitudes spread quicker and easier than positive attitudes. All of us have the ability to jump on the negative band wagon. It is part of our sin nature, our flesh.

We also see that negativity is a group sport. Negative people don't like to be negative alone. It's no fun! It is as though we become like "piranha people" feeding frantically on the negative idea until it is completely devoured.

The fear and panic were so strong that the people became paranoid and began to talk of conspiracy. In verse three they ask, "Why is the Lord bringing us to this land only to let us fall by the sword?" They saw Moses in collusion with God in a grand conspiracy theory. What a slap in the face for God and Moses when these people they loved said they'd rather be back in Egypt. A coup attempt was already being considered. Where is the belief? Where is the loyalty? Where is the courage?

4. Maybe the grumblers had a point. After all it was THE PROMISED LAND. Do you think they assumed that occupying it should be easier? Why do you think they felt that way?

5. What "promised lands" have you had that were harder to occupy than you expected?

session three

God Responds to Courage and to Cowardice

Read Numbers 14:5-12

These verses represent one of the greatest examples of leadership you'll ever see. At the heights of rebellion and chaos Moses, Aaron, Caleb, and Joshua took a stance that proved stronger than a million angry defectors ... they fell down on their faces! They cried out to God and tore their clothes in grief. They repented on behalf of everyone there. They begged for the favor and intervention of their "co-conspirator," their Heavenly Father. What must the people have been thinking? What could they do with that response from their leaders? What a temptation it must have been for Moses, Aaron, and the two faithful spies to respond from a place of pride. How easy it would have been for them to flex their power or to pout and walk off. Instead they showed great vulnerability as well as complete dependence upon God's power instead of their own.

6. How is the response of these "faith-filled" leaders different from the kind of leadership you have exhibited or been exposed to?

7. Why is this approach to leadership so rare? What core human tendencies have to be overcome to act in this way?

Read Numbers 14:10-35. Keep an eye out for God's response to the cowardice of the crowd.

Like a hero in an action movie, God shows up, guns blazing, right on cue. It was as if He was saying to the faithful four; "I've got your back boys." We see that God is attracted to this paradoxical blend of courage and humility, for it took both as they fell on their faces before God.

There they all were on the edge of the promised blessing. They could smell the promised land, but God said, "No! You're not going in." He sent them away making them pay in like kind and in proportion with the width and depth of their rebellion. The sentence: One year of wandering in the desert for each day that He had shown them His promise and they had turned their noses up at the offer—40 years! God made it very clear that He had shown them enough of His power for them to believe. He had helped them come out on top in enough overwhelming battles for them to find courage to face this enemy. It was the smallness of their faith, not the size of the giants of Anak that caused their courage to shrivel. Their spiritual eyes were closed to the promised blessing represented by the massive cluster of grapes. All they could see was the opposition from the foe.

8. Does God's response seem fair and reasonable to you? Why didn't He just perform some great miracle right then to give them enough faith to go forward?

9. Have there been times in your own experience where you feel like God has sent you "back to the desert" for a time of correction and preparation? What was the result in your life?

Another Chance and Another Call to Courage

Read Joshua 1:1-9

Let's fast forward about 40 years and see how courage is rewarded. The

session three

Israelites are once again perched on the edge of the promised land. It is like déjà vu all over again … only different. This time there was a whole new group of courageous leaders with two Medal of Valor winners, Joshua and Caleb, in the lead. All the other rebellious adults had died in the wilderness, never tasting the promised land.

God was preparing to stand by His word and transfer the deed to the land. Even though the group that stood before Him had shown their metal in the desert, learning discipline and obedience, He still pulled them aside and challenged them to take courage. We never have enough. Even receiving what God had promised was going to require incredible courage.

10. Why does God repeat his command, "Be strong and courageous," so many times?

11. What does Israel's 40-year attitude makeover say about the nature of God's heart and His priorities?

Lift It Up

Sometimes we feel like we've made too many cowardly decisions in our lives to see ourselves as people of courage. But God doesn't change His view quite so easily. Consider the example of Simon Peter in Matthew 26:31-35. He told Jesus that no matter what, he would stand with Him and be a man of courage. He didn't. He actually collapsed his courage and avoided his own "promised land." But we read later in John 21:15-19 that Jesus completely reinstated Peter after his cowardly acts, and built him up to lead and encourage others in their struggles.

session three

12. In what area of your life do you need to be strong and courageous? Why do you feel anxious or fearful?

Pray for each other that you will be filled with courage to enter into the place God is leading you. Be honest about the "giants" and "fortified cities" you see that stand in your way. As you pray, borrow courage from the people who stand with you.

My Prayer Needs:

_____
_____
_____
_____
_____

My Group's Prayer Needs:

_____
_____
_____
_____
_____
_____
_____
_____
_____
_____

DEVOTIONALS

A Race to Finish

Day 1

"And now, compelled by the Spirit, I am going to Jerusalem, not knowing what will happen to me there. I only know that in every city the Holy Spirit warns me that prison and hardships are facing me. However, I consider my life worth nothing to me, if only I may finish the race and complete the task the Lord Jesus has given me—the task of testifying to the gospel of God's grace." (Acts 20:22-24)

One of the secrets to Paul's boldness was his unwavering belief that God would finish what He started. It was as if Paul was saying, "This was all Your idea so finish it how You want to."

There are times in our spiritual walk when we realize we are clearly doing what God wants. And therefore—win, lose, or draw—all that matters is that life plays out the way He wants it to.

In every endeavor there are parts that we can't control and God won't control. God will not guarantee our active obedience; He releases that to us. On the flip side, we can't guarantee the outcome of our labor; we need to release outcomes to Him.

What does God want you to do today in your work life? Family life? Social Life? Spiritual Life? Will you trust Him with the outcomes, not knowing what will happen to you?

_____

_____

_____

_____

_____

DEVOTIONALS

Courage to Approach God

Day 2

Then Abraham approached him and said: "Will you sweep away the righteous with the wicked? ... Far be it from you! Will not the Judge of all the earth do right?" (Genesis 18:23,25b)

It takes great courage to approach a living, powerful God with complete candor and honesty. As Abraham interceded for the city of Sodom he confessed his confusion and internal conflict about God's plans to destroy the city.

As we read on in the passage, it reveals an interesting thing about God's character. Though He is unchanging, He is flexible. He is touched by a righteous, compassionate heart that is willing to stand in the gap for the innocent. Abraham found the soft place in God's heart. He also learned something about the heart of God. He has a great capacity for honest, courageous conversation with His obedient children.

How would you pray differently if you approached God with more candor and honesty?

_____

_____

_____

_____

_____

_____

_____

_____

_____

DEVOTIONALS

Boldness of the Righteous

Day 3

The wicked man flees though no one pursues, but the righteous are as bold as a lion. (Proverbs 28:1)

Someone has said, "When you always tell the truth, you don't have to have a good memory." You don't have to worry about lies catching up with you. You can walk with confidence.

If you are feeling tentative, afraid, or worried today, check to see if you might have some unconfessed sin or concealed rebellion against God in your life. Even having a broken relationship with a person in your life can cause you to feel unsure in your stride. Make it right and feel the confidence surge inside of you.

God will reveal any concealed sin, if you will ask Him. So ask Him, deal with it, and move on.

Are you feeling as bold as a lion? If not, are there areas of sin or unresolved conflict that might be hindering you?

_____

_____

_____

_____

_____

_____

_____

_____

_____

DEVOTIONALS

Confidence in Approaching God's Throne

Day 4

Let us then approach the throne of grace with confidence, so that we may receive mercy and find grace to help us in our time of need. (Hebrews 4:16)

One of the great values of close, long-term relationships is assurance that those who know us so well still love us deeply. These kinds of earthly relationships give us a glimpse of the reality that we are able to experience with God.

Think about this: An all-knowing God who sits on His throne, sees parts of you that even you don't see clearly, yet He loves you thousands of times more than your dearest friend.

God has gone to great lengths so that you can know that He understands you, loves you, and wants you to approach Him often. He truly wants to surround you with His mercy and grace, but He also wants you to come boldly to Him to receive these blessings.

How often do you think of God's throne as a throne of grace, rather than as a throne of judgment? How much of God's mercy and grace are you are missing out on because you have not fully grasped God's incredible love for you?

_____

_____

_____

_____

_____

DEVOTIONALS

Loveless Fear

Day 5

There is no fear in love. But perfect love drives out fear, because fear has to do with punishment. The one who fears is not made perfect in love. (1 John 4:18)

Nothing erodes our confidence like the feeling that we are under a debt we can never pay. Our enemy, Satan works constantly to undercut our confidence with a "wait 'til your Dad gets home" lie. He wants to instill in us a fear of our heavenly Father—a nagging dread that we can never give enough to make up for our sin.

The ironclad promise to all of us who have chosen to follow Christ and are filled with God's perfect love is this: the debt is paid in full! We will owe nothing when we stand before God! We will be free to worship Him. Ask God today to fill you so full of His love that there will not be room for anything else.

Have you fully accepted your "paid in full" receipt? What are some ways that you can more fully internalize God's perfect love for you?

_____

_____

_____

_____

_____

_____

_____

_____

DEVOTIONALS

Complete Love

Day 6

Love the LORD your God with all your heart and with all your soul and with all your strength. (Deuteronomy 6:5)

Because of the sin stain on our lives, we can't love purely. But when Jesus came to die on the cross, He was coming to wash away the stain of sin. So, if we want to love others well, we must start by learning to love God. As we love Him and experience His love working in us, it will overflow to the people around us.

Our capacity to love deeply and completely is marred by sin. God works tirelessly to restore that in us, not because He needs us to love Him, but because we need to love Him to be complete. Our love for God is the key to everything else that really matters.

Ask God today to take inventory in your life and see where your love for Him could have a greater grip on your life.

How are you doing at loving the Lord with your whole heart? How could you do a better job of loving the people around you?

_____

_____

_____

_____

_____

_____

_____

DEVOTIONALS

Circumcised Heart

Day 7

To the LORD your God belong the heavens, even the highest heavens, the earth and everything in it. Yet the LORD set his affection on your forefathers and loved them, and he chose you, their descendants, above all the nations, as it is today. Circumcise your hearts, therefore, and do not be stiff-necked any longer. (Deuteronomy 10:14-16)

God doesn't hang around you because He doesn't "have a life." He chooses to love you. He hasn't been tricked into it and He didn't make a snap decision. He has been loving people since long before you arrived.

In the Old Testament, circumcision was an outward sign of God's people's commitment to Him. But God reminded His people that what He wanted most was an inward mark on their hearts—evidenced by their obedience. "Stiff-necked" rebellion showed a heart condition that needed treatment.

If we are honest, most of us have been disappointed by God at some time. A devastating, yet predictable, human response to disappointment is to build up protection and resistance in our hearts. This results in rebellion. Ask the Lord to cleanse your heart of all impurity.

How does it make you feel that God chooses to love you and created you so that He could lavish His love on you? What rooms in your life need a little cleaning out?

_____

_____

_____

_____

_____

DEVOTIONALS

Divine Protection

Day 8

"Because he loves me," says the LORD, "I will rescue him; I will protect him, for he acknowledges my name. He will call upon me, and I will answer him; I will be with him in trouble, I will deliver him and honor him. With long life will I satisfy him and show him my salvation." (Psalm 91:14-16)

Those in love with and fully devoted to God enter into a powerful contract. When God signed on the dotted line, He obligated all of heaven's resources to come to the aid of those of us who love Him.

Of course, we must balance this statement with Jesus' promise that "in this world you will have trouble." So it isn't that we won't experience pain and disappointment, but rather, that we won't experience it alone. And we will not experience ultimate defeat because God has promised His protection.

Our part of the contract is to learn to love God more and more throughout our lives. What a privilege!

Can you truly say that you love God and are devoted to Him? Is it obvious to others around you and to God? Thank God for His heavenly protection.

_____

_____

_____

_____

_____

DEVOTIONALS

Love for the Lord Who Hears

Day 9

I love the LORD, for he heard my voice; he heard my cry for mercy. Because he turned his ear to me, I will call on him as long as I live. (Psalm 116:1-2)

Have you ever been in a crowded, noisy room trying to listen to someone and found it exhausting? Fortunately for us, He has the desire and the capacity to listen to His entire creation at the same time.

Few things cause us to feel more cared about than having someone listen to us. Not just to endure us, but to really enjoy everything that we are saying. It may be hard for us sometimes to believe that God really hears us. That is probably the reason why he jammed the entire Bible with stories and accounts of people communicating with Him.

There are several benefits to us understanding and believing we are getting through to God. Among them, and possibly most important, is that we will get in the habit of talking with Him, knowing that our communication is wanted and valued.

Ask God to check your heart today to see where your belief level is. Do you really think God is hearing every word you say? Acknowledge your belief and ask Him to help you with your unbelief.

_____

_____

_____

_____

_____

DEVOTIONALS

God's Loving Purposes

Day 10

And we know that in all things God works for the good of those who love him, who have been called according to his purpose. (Romans 8:28)

Have you ever been irritated by this verse? Too often it is quoted by someone with a saccharin grin and a dripping religious, patronizing tone at a time when you are at the end of your rope.

Without careful examination, we head off in the wrong direction with this verse. We can develop the mistaken idea that every problem or challenge is going to turn out okay, which we know from experience is not true. Most of us have had enough disappointment or even tragedy in our lives to know that the good guy doesn't always win.

But this verse doesn't say that. It says that through God's love for us, He will stay engaged in every circumstance in your life, making sure that something good can come from it. God's love and power guarantee that every life experience, regardless of how painful, can have a deeper, greater purpose in your life. Invite Him fully into your journey today to work out His purposes.

Are you trusting God's purposes for your life, even when things are difficult?

_____
_____
_____
_____
_____
_____

Is God's Love Overflowing in You?

Hosea 1 – 3; 1 John 4:4-19

Love is clearly one of the most talked about, sought after, and misunderstood character qualities in all of Scripture. Love is central to who God is, in fact "God is Love" as 1 John 4:8 reveals. His actions throughout history define love. It's not the fluffy stuff of Valentine's Day cards and chocolate. It's tough, gritty, and sometimes controversial.

As we pull back the curtain on an Old Testament love story, we find it filled with sin, betrayal, and incredible reconciliation. We see God unfold a real-life drama to communicate a kind of love that drives us to our knees in disbelief, gratitude, and adoration.

This love story of a man named Hosea and his unfaithful wife, Gomer, reveals God's heart of love for the rebellious children of Israel ... and at the same time His heart of patient love for each of us who follow Him today. Their love story was very real, but God planned it to paint a picture of His love relationship with us today.

Start It Up

Love can be an incredible experience. It can also be deeply painful.

1. Do you remember your first love? How did you feel when you were around him/her?

58

2. What was the first time you remember giving love to someone (or something) when it wasn't reciprocated?

Talk It Up

You might expect this stop on our Character Tour to be the most enchanting and heart-warming, but it may instead be the most difficult and heart-rending. After this stop we are going to know what true love is all about. We are going to see ourselves in this love story and we probably aren't going to like what we see. We are, however, going to love what we see about God.

Hosea was called to prophesy judgment against Israel at a time when things were going pretty well for them, at least from their point of view. Since they were feeling so good, it was going to take something dramatic from God to get their attention. They needed to know two things: (1) they would be experiencing judgment for their rebellion, and (2) God was pursuing them for meaningful and intimate relationship.

An Unfaithful and Ungrateful Lover

Read Hosea 1:1-11

From the very beginning, Hosea must have known that this wasn't going to be your typical fairy-tale love story. He was commanded to begin a relationship with a woman who already had a far less than perfect reputation. That love story should sound familiar because it mimics God's love for us. In Romans 5:8 we read, "But God demonstrates his own love for us in this: While we were still sinners, Christ died for us." He loves us even though we are far less than perfect.

3. Why do you think God had Hosea marry an adulteress? How does this fit with God's view of marriage in general?

True Love's Faithful Pursuit

Read Hosea 2:2-5

Put yourself in Hosea's sandals. He married one of the most beautiful women in the land. With a name like Gomer, she had to be gorgeous! Then suddenly and without any warning she just splits. Even though Hosea had shown such patience and love during her unfaithfulness to him in their marriage, now she turns and leaves.

One of the things we are going to see in this story is that when we try to run from God, we end up running right into His embrace. We have all "gone Gomer" in one way or another in our lives. But even though we don't deserve it, God loves us. In fact, He's crazy about us, so He pursues us and woos us back to Himself.

4. Hosea pursued Gomer and she just kept running. When we run from God and refuse to turn back, what does He do? What have you seen him do in your life?

session four

Read Hosea 2:6-13

God responded to Gomer's unfaithful rebellion in a loving and decisive way. There were three tactics He used to stop the cycle of self-destruction. As we study these, think about how God works in our lives today.

Thorny Turnabout Tactic

As Hosea 2:6 indicates, the first thing God does in our rebellion is to barricade us with thorn bushes. Recently, my family and I went hiking and made our way down through a path, deep into the woods. We skipped rocks on a lake and enjoyed the beauty and relaxation of our natural surroundings. We soon realized that it was getting late and we needed to head back. Even though I am directionally challenged, I urged, "follow me, I'll lead the way." Instead of leading us out, I led us right into a briar patch. The thorns were scratching and digging into our skin. Trying to push through created more pain and groaning. We were stuck and our path was blocked by the thorn bushes. Finally, we decided to turn around and head the opposite direction. After turning from the thorny path, we found the right path and made it back to our truck.

When we run from God and pursue sin, as Gomer did, He barricades us with thorn bushes and it can be painful. We experience the consequences of our chosen path. Because of God's love, He can't let us go without trying to turn us around. He begins to wall us in so we can't find our way and hopes we will turn back to Him soon.

5. How do you imagine Gomer experienced the "thorns" as she was running away?

6. What is an example of how God has barricaded you with "thorny bushes" in your life?

Ruthless Resource Removal

Even painful thorn bushes aren't enough to stop us sometimes. They certainly didn't stop Gomer. Hosea 2:7-8 indicates that she continued to pursue her lovers. But they eluded her.

When the thorn bushes didn't work, God upped the ante. Hosea 2:9 describes how He ruthlessly removed all her resources. Up until that point at least her daily needs were being met. Gomer was suddenly in serious trouble. She was in debt. She had many miles on her, yet she had no place to go. She was unfaithful and unrepentant. The Bible portrays her as suffering, financially broke, busted, and disgusted.

7. Why did Hosea quit providing for her? What do you think was His motivation?

Gomer was so desperate that she sold herself into slavery. The slave auctions were a terrible, dehumanizing experience. She had to strip naked and stand there in front of a bunch a people while they bid on her. It seemed that Gomer had finally hit bottom—forced to sell herself as a slave in her quest for freedom. The irony is painful and yet true for all of us today. We have all "gone Gomer" in one way or another. This depiction is a disgusting, yet accurate illustration of the progressive destruction that sin can cause in our lives.

8. What must Gomer have been feeling about her life and choices at this point? When you sin and rebel against God, how do you feel afterwards?

God's Grip of Grace

Read Hosea 3:1-3

This all-time low in Gomer's rebellion set up the third tactic that we see God use to bring us back to Him. He grips us with His grace. You probably could have knocked Hosea over with a feather when God said, "Go show your wife your love again"—essentially, "go buy your wife back and restore her." Who wouldn't be surprised if Hosea thought that was a stupid idea? Most of us would have huge objections! You can picture Hosea standing at the back of the crowd saying to himself, "I can't believe I am going to do this." And there stood Gomer preparing herself to be sold as a soiled and broken piece of property. She had no idea that her faithful redeemer stood at the back of the crowd ready to purchase her freedom. If you are a sucker for good endings, this story has one.

Hosea, representing the love of God for His wayward children, stepped to the front, laid down his pride as well as his hard-earned cash, and amazingly ... gave Gomer her life back.

9. What part of this process do you think was most difficult for Hosea? What would be the hardest part for you if you were in this position?

Lift It Up

This stop on our Character Tour has been difficult, and yet there is such incredible hope in the fact that God loves us beyond our wildest hopes and imaginations. As we truly grasp and accept God's amazing love, it is His love that will overflow from our lives, affecting everyone around us. 1 John 4:7,19 explains, "Let us love one another, for love comes from God. Everyone who loves has been born of God and knows God. ... We love because he first loved us." We see again that our character is the outward reflection of our inward connection.

10. What are some things that you can do to help one another remain faithful to God or to help each other turn back to God in times of rebellion?

11. Is it easy or difficult for you to accept God's amazing love? What does the Bible mean that "we love because He first loved us"?

Take a few minutes in prayer acknowledging God's awesome character and deep love for you that will not let go! Pray that God's love will flood your heart and overflow out of your life, dramatically affecting everyone you come in contact with.

My Prayer Needs:

_____

_____

_____

_____

_____

My Group's Prayer Needs:

_____

_____

_____

_____

_____

_____

_____

_____

_____

_____

_____

DEVOTIONALS

Life in Unity

Day 1

How good and pleasant it is when brothers live together in unity! (Psalm 133:1)

David, the writer of this Psalm, had to flee from King Saul and lived with major conflict even in his own family. So, he could really appreciate how good it is when everyone gets along!

He knew we were made for community. Our connection with other people puts things in order and prepares the way for many other benefits in our life.

David touches on these benefits with the word, "pleasant." It means lovely, charming, and attractive; that which fills the mind with delight. Few things are more attractive than diverse, unique people going through life together. Though we were made for such connections, most of us have a hard time really connecting with others.

As tempting as it is go it alone at times, remember that we were designed to make it through life together.

Who can you call today to either repair a damaged relationship or advance a healthy one? What can you do to live in unity with others, especially other Christians?

_____

_____

_____

_____

DEVOTIONALS

Covered Offenses

Day 2

He who covers over an offense promotes love, but whoever repeats the matter separates close friends. (Proverbs 17:9)

Grace motivates us to continuously shorten our "short list" of non-negotiables in our friendships. You know, that list of things that you just cannot overlook—those little "idiot-syncrasies" we all possess. There is such power and grace in choosing to close our mouths. Well-positioned silence can sometimes communicate love better than well-spoken words.

Choosing to overlook things in other people's lives takes a great deal of faith. Faith that God will get their attention if a change needs to be made. And, faith that they will have the desire to make the changes God identifies.

Ask God to help you discipline your mouth today and bless your friends with your well-positioned silence. Choose to be an encourager rather than a discourager. There are enough people spreading discouragement already.

Are you a discourager or an encourager? What are some relationships in your life that could use more well-positioned silence?

_____

_____

_____

_____

_____

_____

_____

DEVOTIONALS

Extra Miles

Day 3

"If someone forces you to go one mile, go with him two miles."
(Matthew 5:41)

In a day of exact measures and unrelenting competition it seems extremely impractical, if not completely foolish, to allow another person to "put one over on you," like this verse describes. After all, aren't we taught to stand up for ourselves? Doesn't society insist that we fight for our rights?

Okay, it's true! There are many people in this world who would hurt you if you let them. You do need discernment to stand against those who would enslave you. And this is precisely Jesus' point! Choosing to go the extra mile is a loud, bold statement of personal freedom. You choose the extra mile. You are in control!

Of course Jesus had full credibility to teach this principle. No one in history so willingly chose to go the extra mile. He said in John 10:18, "No one takes it [my life] from me, but I lay it down of my own accord."

The good news is that through the Holy Spirit, this "extra mile" love is available to all of us. Each of us can choose the extra mile.

How can you lay down your agenda and go the extra mile for somebody else?

_____

_____

_____

_____

_____

DEVOTIONALS

Foot Washing

Day 4

"Now that I, your Lord and Teacher, have washed your feet, you also should wash one another's feet." (John 13:14-15)

What did Jesus do by washing the feet of His disciples? He completely turned the first century system of power and authority on its head. He displayed a love with the power to break down barriers and level the ground so that all stand as one.

Jesus possessed the perfect love talked about in Scripture. He had no concern about how this serving posture would make Him look. He wasn't afraid of being taken advantage of. He wasn't worried that He would lose His position as a leader and teacher. He was fully overtaken by a deep love and desire to serve others.

Imagine the amount of growth that would take place in our lives if we loved like that! Think about how relaxed we would be if we were not concerned with how we looked to others. What if we believed that selfless acts of serving love were more important than selfish acts of self-promotion!

What attitudes do you need God to change to enable you to serve others like your Lord and Teacher does?

_____

_____

_____

_____

_____

DEVOTIONALS

Command to Love

Day 5

"This is my command: Love each other." (John 15:17)

We tend to look at love as an elective, rather than a requirement. We do not often think about the command to love. The truth is, our refusal to love those around us is an act of rebellion against God with serious spiritual repercussions.

Why did Jesus make it a command instead of just a really good suggestion? He knew that until we were able to love others, including the unlovely, we would never really know Him.

It is through learning to love the undeserving that we begin to believe that it might actually be true that God is able to love us in our sinful and incomplete state.

Jesus went on to define the standard of love by His own testimony. The thing that He made abundantly clear is this: love is not real love unless it is selfless love.

Confess your difficulty of loving like Jesus and ask Him to love through you today.

_____

_____

_____

_____

_____

_____

DEVOTIONALS

Image of the Creative God

Day 6

In the beginning God created the heavens and the earth. ... So God created man in his own image, in the image of God he created him; male and female he created them. (Genesis 1:1,27)

Put these two verses together and you have an interesting question. Since we are created in God's image and He is the creator of the world; how much of His creative capacity is living within us?

I haven't created any new animals lately, have you? Yet God has placed within each of us a huge desire to see new things. God created Adam and Eve and then invited them to be fully engaged in His creative activity.

Just like Adam and Eve, we are called to engage in His creative purposes. Every new day is an opportunity to create. Every new relationship begs for creative imagination. Each disagreement with our teenager or spouse provides a place for creative initiative.

View yourself today as part of God's creative team. With every new challenge, pause for a moment and check in with God and ask Him what He wants to create in that moment.

In which area(s) of your life are you most creative? In which area do you most need help from the master Creator?

_____

_____

_____

_____

_____

DEVOTIONALS

A New Creation

Day 7

Therefore, if anyone is in Christ, he is a new creation; the old has gone, the new has come! (2 Corinthians 5:17)

When we become a Christ-follower, there is a brand new capacity for life that is made available to us. There is a new way of thinking and new eyes for seeing God's activity in the world.

The most significant change is the transforming of our vision of what is real. In the process of learning what it means to be new, we are now able to see our lives and our world through different eyes. We begin to see how God really sees us. We can now see a way out from old habits that once bound us. Relationships that were stuck in "Nowhere Ville" have new vistas open. Limitations in our own abilities now melt away inside the power of God.

Be careful not to miss the secret to this new vision. It is being "in Christ." New life comes through continuous connection with the God who now lives in us. Do you want to be able to see and create new possibilities in your life, challenges, and relationships? To make this happen, your most important task is to be sure that you regularly spend time with Him.

How much of this "new creation" life are you experiencing? What steps can you take to walk away from the old and toward the new?

_____

_____

_____

_____

DEVOTIONALS

Recreated Heart

Day 8

Create in me a pure heart, O God, and renew a steadfast spirit within me. (Psalm 51:10)

The most impressive accomplishment on God's resume is not creating the sun, mammals, or even woman out of a man's rib. The most impressive entry is that He can make our hearts new and clean, day after day.

David, who wrote this Psalm, asked for this powerful act of creation. Given what he had just dragged his heart through in adultery and murder, he knew that his heart needed more than just a brushing off.

God's approach to hearts is like a core exchange at an auto parts store. You take in your old starter motor to exchange it for a rebuilt one. When they rebuild starters they are able to use the same casing, but completely replace the moving parts inside. So it is with our hearts. If we want a new heart, we need to bring in our old one for exchange and rebuilding.

Regardless of how much you have banged up or abused your heart, you can bring Him that old one today and do a "core exchange."

Honestly assess your heart condition. As you confess your failings and sins to God, what areas does He need to recreate and restore in your heart?

_____

_____

_____

_____

_____

DEVOTIONALS

Wellspring of Life

Day 9

Above all else, guard your heart, for it is the wellspring of life. (Proverbs 4:23)

Have you ever been on a hike, hot and tired from the physical exertion of climbing up a never-ending incline? After a long day of hiking, there is nothing like a drink from a natural spring in the mountains! On a hot summer day, this water that flows from deep under the earth's surface is refreshing and rejuvenating. It is untainted and untouched.

Our hearts are intended to be like a freshwater spring. They are meant to be a source of life and strength when we are facing the never-ending challenges of life. But they can become contaminated with a lot of garbage. When they do, they no longer give us energy. Suddenly, we find ourselves completely drained and running on empty.

We need to guard our hearts to keep them pure and clean—running efficiently so they can provide the endurance we need. God can do that in your heart today. Ask Him to rule over the inner workings of your heart so that it may continue to flow with His creative power.

How well are you guarding your heart and maintaining that "wellspring of life"? What areas do you need to give to God for cleansing and healing?

_____

_____

_____

_____

DEVOTIONALS

Christ's Ambassadors

Day 10

We are therefore Christ's ambassadors, as though God were making his appeal through us. (2 Corinthians 5:20a)

Nothing challenges our creative imagination more than being involved in God's ongoing search-and-rescue mission. This passage doesn't leave us any options. We are Christ's ambassadors. We may not be active or effective, but we are on His payroll nonetheless.

If you are looking to be stretched, ask God what His game plan is for creating a bridge to the heart of your coworker. If you really want to be stretched, ask Him how he intends to create a lifeline with your neighbor.

God initiated the entire creation event so that He would have His own people to love and bless. Yet there are so many people around us who have built walls or dug motes around their hearts. God won't give up on the task of creating new bridges into the hearts of men and women.

If you are at the end of your ideas and resources for communicating the love of God to people in your world ... good! This is the perfect time to access the creative genius of the Holy Spirit at work in you and ask for new ideas.

What kind of ambassador are you for Christ? Where do you need to focus on reaching out with His creativity and power?

_____

_____

_____

_____

Are You Riding the Crest of Creativity?

Genesis 1; Matthew 13:34; 2 Corinthians 3:16-18

Our Character Tour stop today is with a quality that wouldn't make most of our lists for character qualities. In fact if you do a Google® search for "character qualities" on the Internet, "creativity" doesn't even show up.

Creativity is part of God's framework and is woven into the very fabric of who He is. Though it doesn't make most of our character quality lists, it is foundational to the life of a Christ-follower. For some, every time you hear the word "creativity," you squirm and then release a rush of reasons why you are not more creative. Or maybe you think of other people in your life and say, "now *they* are creative … not me."

All of us are born with a massive capacity for creative genius that we seldom tap into. Of course, we're not all wired with the same type or level of creativity, but somewhere along the way many of us leave the path blazed by our Creator and begin to trudge in the rut of sameness and predictability. We reason, "That's just the way it is. I just have to live my life in a world of predictability. I'll just splash around in the shallows of sameness with my floaters on."

Start It Up

Each of us has some level of creativity. It may not stand out in the forefront of our lives, but it's there if we look.

session five

1. What are some areas or activities where you are more creative?

2. If you had unlimited funding and you knew you couldn't fail, what would you like to invent?

Talk It Up

Our God is both the author of creativity and of order. To us, the two seem mutually exclusive, but not so with God. So, hang on! He wants you to ride on the crest of creativity—to be on the cutting edge. He wants you to go for creative growth in your marriage, in your career, with your family, and with your friends. Regardless of your individual design and bent, He wants you to be free to mimic the creativity inherent in His character. We don't have to look very far to find creativity in the Bible.

Creative Origins

God kick-started creativity in Genesis 1:1—"In the beginning, God created ..." God is all about creativity. Our world and humanity began with it, literally! It is stamped into His identity and because of that, it is stamped into your life and mine.

Genesis 1:26 says, "Let us make man in our image, in our likeness." Because of that statement we can be assured that all us have the ability to be creative. As His image bearers, we carry His creative thumbprint, as well as His ability to live an ordered life.

3. Do you think we were all given the same amount of creativity? If not, why did God give more creativity to some than others?

Just look through the pages of Scripture and you'll see the creative genius of God. He used a piece of fruit to communicate something of eternal significance to Adam and Eve. You see God using the hair of Samson to communicate that it is His power that matters in our lives. He used a huge boat to communicate His mercy and justice to Noah. A slingshot is what He used to create a life-changing message with David. At the pinnacle of human history, He used an old rugged cross and an empty burial tomb to deliver the most significant creative object lesson of all time.

4. Why do you think God has been so committed to creative communication techniques throughout history? Wouldn't it have been enough for Him to just thunder His voice from heaven?

5. Which of these creative object lessons given in the Bible holds the most personal meaning for you?

session five

SMALL-GROUP SESSION

Creative Embodiment

As surely as the Father was the origin of creativity, the Son continuously modeled and still models it. When Jesus lived on earth, He preached from beaches and bows of boats. He drew in the sand. He picked up a seed and taught a lesson with it in His hands. He pointed to a building and spoke of His authority to tear down and build back up. He picked up a coin and taught about authority. He pulled a child on to His lap and gave an incredible lesson on kingdom status and faith. His first object lesson revealed His miraculous power and generous love when he turned your basic H_2O into first-rate Merlot to help His mother at a wedding.

Read Matthew 13:34. Jesus used creativity in the form of parables as His primary style of teaching and influencing people.

6. How can you apply Jesus' methods in the places you are called to be a spiritual influence?

Creative Empowerment

The Father originates creativity, the Son models it, and the Holy Spirit empowers it. Remember in earlier sessions we said that our character is the outward reflection of our inward connection. This character pathway is how we make our way into the arena of creativity—from the inside out. When we meet the King of creativity, He implants the Holy Spirit in our lives to develop Christ-likeness in every aspect, and that includes reaching our creative potential. The Holy Spirit was involved in our world's creation, in the beautiful craftsmanship for the Old Testament temple, and in giving diverse spiritual gifts to members of the New Testament church. That same Spirit lives and works in you!

session five

Read 2 Corinthians 3:16-18

Have you ever asked yourself the question, "how can I be more creative?" Many of us have asked the question. Yet, it's not the right question, even though the goal is valid. The better question is, "God, what is blocking the creativity that is already a part of me?" We need to have our "veil" taken away, freeing us in this area so that we can reflect the glory of our Creator.

7. What is it that blocks your creativity?

8. In what area of your life (marriage, parenting, business, ministry, personal growth, etc.) do you feel the biggest need for increased creativity?

9. What changes do you need to make to increase creativity in that area? What could happen as your creativity grows?

Lift It Up

As we look forward to experiencing increased creativity in our lives, we must start by asking for God's help.

10. In which of these three areas do you struggle the most?
    - Desire for more creativity
    - Strategy for carrying out creativity
    - Commitment to continuous creativity

11. What are some ways that you, individually and as a group, can become more intentional about developing creativity in your lives?

Pray for each other and ask God to awaken you to your creative potential.

My Prayer Needs:

_____

_____

_____

_____

_____

My Group's Prayer Needs:

_____

_____

_____

_____

_____

_____

_____

_____

DEVOTIONALS

Spirit of Power

Day 1

For God did not give us a spirit of timidity, but a spirit of power, of love and of self-discipline. (2 Timothy 1:7)

Timothy was evidently feeling a little wobbly in his faith. A young man of his age and relative lack of experience may have felt unqualified or unprepared for his leadership assignment.

Paul was reminding him that when we quit or cower, it really is a matter of mistaken identity. These are not part of our DNA as believers in Christ. How good it is for Timothy that Paul didn't say, "Hey Tim, I see what you are lacking and it is only going to take a few years of schooling to get it." Everything he needed was already a part of him—available in his spirit.

Each of us has different situations that make us want to run and hide. It sometimes takes a miracle of God to make us stand firm on our wobbly legs. But, part of discipline is learning to stick it out even when we feel like we aren't up for the challenge.

Ask God to remind you of the Spirit that He has placed within you to counter any timid or anxious feelings you are having.

What kinds of situations are you facing right now that cause you to feel stupid or incapable? How can you "fan the flame" of God's Spirit within you as you respond to your circumstances?

_____

_____

_____

_____

DEVOTIONALS

The Prize

Day 2

Run in such a way as to get the prize. (1 Corinthians 9:24b)

When the Bible says to "run in such a way as to get the prize," you probably see a runner forcing his arms and legs forward in machine-like motions. A good track coach will teach you that to run your best, every part of your body needs to work together. The best sprinters even harness the energy from their faces and necks.

In other words, each part affects every other part. This is certainly true in the area of discipline. One new discipline, regardless of how small, can start a chain reaction to another. For example, if you start going to bed on time, you are more likely to start waking earlier in the morning.

Just as it is true in the positive, it's also true in the negative. One lack of discipline can lead to another as well. If your face starts to tighten up when you are running, your shoulders will be next, then your forearms, and so on.

Each new day provides an opportunity to start a new discipline or strengthen an old one. Don't give in to the idea that only the big ones count.

Remembering the principle of the face in sprinting, what one small thing could you do today for God that would get you going in the right direction?

_____

_____

_____

_____

_____

DEVOTIONALS

Living Sacrifices

Day 3

Therefore, I urge you, brothers, in view of God's mercy, to offer your bodies as living sacrifices, holy and pleasing to God—this is your spiritual act of worship. Do not conform any longer to the pattern of this world, but be transformed by the renewing of your mind. Then you will be able to test and approve what God's will is—his good, pleasing and perfect will. (Romans 12:1-2)

Wouldn't it be easier if this verse just read, "offer your Sundays to God" instead of "offer your bodies"? The original readers realized that "body" was referring to their entire life, head-to-toe, offered up to God.

The Apostle Paul knew that the relentless pushing of the world, the devil, and our sinful flesh would attach to every area of a person's life. J.B. Philips' translation says it clearly: "Don't let the world squeeze you into its mold."

Paul's call is for total transformation. Nothing else will come anywhere close to leading us into the life with God that we hope for. But, total transformation means we have to get serious about following God in every area of life. It's not enough to know what God says, but we must also apply and embrace the truth we learn so we can experience this transformation.

As you reread these verses in Romans 12 and allow them to settle into your soul, how should these words alter your life today? What area(s) of life is God showing you that need total transformation?

_____

_____

_____

_____

DEVOTIONALS
God's Voice

Day 4

He said, "If you listen carefully to the voice of the LORD your God and do what is right in his eyes, if you pay attention to his commands and keep all his decrees, I will not bring on you any of the diseases I brought on the Egyptians, for I am the LORD, who heals you." (Exodus 15:26)

God never does anything just to give us something to do. Every one of His commands has a purpose. Those purposes are rooted in His amazing love for us, as He constantly works to bless us with all good things.

The hard road of discipline and obedience has great rewards. In this passage God unveils a clear two-point plan: listen and do.

"Listen carefully" and "pay attention" are the first part of the plan. Deep listening is an acquired skill. But it's important because it helps us hear the speaker's heart—the words behind the words.

The next part of the plan is to "do what is right." Don't just hear the information that He is passing along, but do it! Apply it to your life. When we "listen and do" God gives us an awesome promise: We will be free from the devastating results of sin that plague the world around us.

How well have you been really listening to God lately? What steps can you take to improve your deep listening?

_____

_____

_____

_____

DEVOTIONALS

Abundant Harvest

Day 5

"If you follow my decrees and are careful to obey my commands, I will send you rain in its season, and the ground will yield its crops and the trees of the field their fruit. ... and the grape harvest will continue until planting, and you will eat all the food you want and live in safety in your land." (Leviticus 26:3-5)

Have you ever played the word association game? Someone says a word and you have to say whatever words come to your mind. Let's try it! When you hear the word "obedience," what words come to your mind?

Maybe you think of words like "restrictions," "rules," "limits." But God wants you to think of words like "blessings," "protection," and "love." When you choose to live God's way, you are choosing to get in line with Him so you can experience all that He wants to pour out on you. God wants to protect you from unnecessary pain and suffering. But, He knows that there are many things in this world, and in us, that will get us off course.

God isn't a cosmic killjoy; He's a loving creator. God could have created us and then left us on our own. But, instead, He loved us enough to give us guidelines for life. When we choose His way, we experience His blessings.

How firmly have you grabbed hold of the principle that God's commands are really for our benefit? In what areas of life are you still holding out your obedience—doing things your own way?

_____

_____

_____

_____

DEVOTIONALS

Obedience and Blessing

Day 6

Oh, that their hearts would be inclined to fear me and keep all my commands always, so that it might go well with them and their children forever! (Deuteronomy 5:29)

As I read this verse, my mind flashes back to those many times that my children caught me reading my Bible as I sat before God in a quiet place. The look of curiosity on their faces was unmistakable. You could almost see them making mental notes: meeting with God ... okay, this is a good thing.

As positive as it is for our children to catch us studying God's commands, it is even more positive for them to catch us obeying them. Nothing makes a larger impression on those around us—be they our children or our friends—than when we follow God's commands in front of them. That's real discipline—not just knowing God's commands, but living them out.

But notice the order of the words "fearing" and "keeping." The key to being able to consistently follow God's rules for living is to have a healthy respect and reverence for Him. When we agree that God deserves to be in charge, it's a lot easier to follow His commands.

What words would you use to describe God? Do these words reflect a healthy respect for Him? Do your actions?

_____

_____

_____

_____

_____

DEVOTIONALS

Hard Choices

Day 7

**"See, I set before you today life and prosperity, death and destruction."
(Deuteronomy 30:15)**

At first this verse might seem pretty harsh. Why does God have to be so extreme? Wouldn't it be more in keeping with a benevolent God to set before us "pretty good" and "kind of bad"? It's a little funny to think about God being mediocre like that, but it is a thought that can creep in at times.

God has no desire to take the edge off, or dull life's corners. God is a radical ruler in the universe and has no interest in mediocre existence. He is not trying to be extreme; He is extreme! Extreme in His love. Extreme in His rightness. Extreme in His sacrifice. And, extreme in His desire to bless us. He lays out the choices plainly and simply. God doesn't live in the lukewarm middle and doesn't want His children there either.

He treats us with great respect in allowing us to choose. He knows we are capable of choosing rightly because He made us. He also knows that we need help to make right decisions with our lives. For that reason, He sent the Holy Spirit to come alongside us and live inside us, so that we will always have the power to choose life.

As you think about your life right now, are you choosing life ... or destruction? What decisions in your life support your answer?

_____

_____

_____

_____

DEVOTIONALS

God's Test

Day 8

"Bring the whole tithe into the storehouse, that there may be food in my house. Test me in this," says the LORD Almighty, "and see if I will not throw open the floodgates of heaven and pour out so much blessing that you will not have room enough for it." (Malachi 3:10)

Nothing tests our level of discipline like money. Our commitment to giving must be rugged in order to push through all of the challenges.

And God is up to challenges. He commands us to challenge Him. It is as if God is saying, "Go ahead; fire a fast pitch down the middle and I'll knock it out of the park." The term "floodgates" paints a picture of an almost frightening amount of blessing. God wants us to see His heart and intention. He wants to create a cycle of trust and reward.

He wants us to see our own hearts as well. He challenges us to bring the "whole tithe." Now that is a heart-check, as well as a gut-check. He doesn't want us to approach giving like putting a quarter in a gum ball machine.

Today you have the opportunity to give your whole life as a sacrifice (the whole tithe) to God. In your relationships, in your challenges, and in your daily interactions with unpredictable life, you can say, "God I am putting it all in the offering plate as it passes by. I trust you with the rest ... let it pour!

How much of your life and wealth are you holding tight to your chest, believing that you know what's best for you? Are you willing to take God's challenge?

_____

_____

DEVOTIONALS

Inheritance

Day 9

We do not want you to become lazy, but to imitate those who through faith and patience inherit what has been promised. (Hebrews 6:12)

I love the story of the little lamb that was enjoying the green grass so much that it didn't even notice that it had wandered out through a hole in the fence. It kept eating and wandering for quite a while until it eventually lifted its head and asked the question many of us ask, "How'd I get here?"

Most of us don't just decide one day that we don't want to follow God anymore—we simply drift. We just stop paying attention. This is exactly what the writer of Hebrews is talking about. Sometimes we get lazy about listening to God's commands, or we just get too busy doing good things.

Instead of drifting, faith gives us the motive to press into God and His Word because we know He will do what He has said. Patience encourages us to realize that God's ways are not our ways and to trust Him to have perfect timing. If we want to have a great inheritance, we will have to allow God to develop great faith and patience in you.

Do you find yourself lazily drifting through life from time to time? What area is God showing you where you need to actively practice faith and patience?

_____

_____

_____

_____

_____

DEVOTIONALS

The Goal

Day 10

I press on to take hold of that for which Christ Jesus took hold of me. Brothers, I do not consider myself yet to have taken hold of it. But one thing I do: Forgetting what is behind and straining toward what is ahead, I press on toward the goal to win the prize for which God has called me heavenward in Christ Jesus. (Philippians 3:12b-14)

The greatest reward of discipline is that you can realize your designed purpose on this planet. Look at the phrase "I press on to take hold of that for which Christ Jesus took hold of me." We all want to know that our life matters. No one wants their tombstone to read: "Lived … died … so what!"

To live a life that matters is all about plugging into our purpose, and Paul gives us two keys. First, we have to be willing to admit that we haven't found it yet—that we are still in process. Secondly, he highlights our need to forget what lies behind us. This encompasses bads and goods. God's grace releases us from past failures; His perfection calls us from past successes.

Make no mistake; Paul points out that there is plenty of strain involved. Here's a good rule of thumb: if your life is too easy for too many days in a row … something is probably wrong. Walking into our destiny is all about walking out of the comfortable and the familiar.

What has God set before you in your race? List below the purpose(s) God has already laid out for you. If you don't know what those purposes are, then ask God to show you.

_____

_____

_____

Has Your Discipline Disintegrated?

Daniel 1:1-17; 6:1-10; 2 Timothy 1:7; Matthew 6:34; Zechariah 4:6

Some time ago I conducted a very informal survey on character qualities. The question I asked was, "If you could name one character quality that you want more of, which quality would it be?"

People thought for a moment and most replied, "You know, what I really need is more discipline." This last stop on our Character Tour takes us to one of the most important, foundational character qualities. It is the one quality that unlocks the expression and fuels the potential of many others.

Just as with our discussion on creativity, when some of you hear the word "discipline," your palms get sweaty and then you toss out a ton of reasons why you're not geared for an ordered life. You reason, "I just can't be a disciplined person. That is reserved for those select few extraordinary people." Well, that is just not true! All of us can go deep with discipline.

Start It Up

Discipline is a common trait among those people who accomplish much in their lives.

1. What is the first thing you remember accomplishing as a young person that took a lot of discipline to complete?

2. In what areas of your life do you find it easiest to be disciplined? Which area is the hardest?

Talk It Up

So, What is Discipline?

Let's start with a working definition: *Discipline is doing what you ought to do so you can do what you want to do.* Many would say, "Okay, I understand the first part ... doing what you ought to do, but I don't understand the second part ... doing what you want to do."

It may seem contradictory to say that discipline actually enables you to do what you want to do. Can that really be discipline? Well it is if you understand it within our definition of character: the outward reflection of our inward connection. When we sync up with God and allow Him to go deep in us, the life of Jesus begins to live through us. In fact, in Paul's first letter to the Corinthian church, he goes so far as to say that we, as Christians with the indwelling of the Holy Spirit, "have the mind of Christ" (1 Corinthians 2:16b). Psalm 37:4 adds, "Delight yourself in the LORD and He will give you the desires of your heart." As we put this together, we recognize that when we allow God to develop His character in us— including discipline—God's desires and perspectives begin to seep into the soil of our life and we begin to want the things that God wants for us.

We already discussed during our stop at creativity that God is both the author of creativity and of order. To us, creativity and discipline may seem mutually exclusive, but not so with God. The word "discipline" in the Bible refers to having soundness of mind or self-control. 2 Timothy 1:7 makes clear that God gave us "a spirit of power, of love and of self-discipline." Regardless of your individual design and bent, God wants you to receive and develop this discipline that He implants in you when you become His child.

session six

A Model of Discipline

Let's look together at a real "character" in the Bible who exhibited this character quality of discipline. Daniel truly stands out as the guy who modeled discipline in some very trying circumstances.

Read Daniel 1:1-17

3. How were these Israelites chosen for service in the king's court? What kind of pressure did this honored selection immediately create?

4. Why was Daniel willing to risk so much in following his commitment not to eat the food that was defiled according to the laws of Moses?

Daniel applied several principles as he went deep with discipline. Before we dive into that, let's get up to speed on Daniel's current situation. Daniel was in Jerusalem with all kinds of friends and enjoying life when King Nebuchadnezzar stormed in from Babylon and messed it all up. Once he had taken over Jerusalem, he carried many back to Babylon. Daniel and his buddies were among that group.

Check this out: Daniel was 800 miles away from home ... by himself. He was a young good-looking guy smack in the middle of a very decadent culture. Old King Neb didn't get to be king because he was a low wattage bulb; he had a brilliant plan. He probably said to himself, "I am going to show these

Jewish people how to really live. I'm gonna fatten them up and give them a taste of the good life!" He wanted them to begin to see the world through his eyes, and then to finally accept his way of life over their own. So he started by laying before them the richest and most decadent foods in the land.

5. What are some things in our culture that threaten to take us away from the obedient, disciplined life God wants us to live?

The Power of Advanced Planning

As Daniel responded to the king's tactic, his secrets for remaining disciplined were revealed. First, he was anchored through advanced planning. Daniel 1:8 says, "But Daniel resolved not to defile himself with the royal food and wine ..." The word for "resolved" is in the past tense in the original Old Testament Hebrew. This means Daniel that had already worked this out in his mind before he reached the point of decision. He was able to show incredible discipline because he had already made up his mind in advance about what was negotiable and what was not.

6. Advanced planning is more than just making up your mind. It is also putting strategies in place to help you avoid temptation. Describe a temptation-defeating strategy you have used or seen used.

session six

Read Daniel 1:9 to see how God responded to Daniel's stand. Notice that it was God who caused the official to show favor and sympathy toward Daniel.

The Power of Connection

The second discipline-builder evident in this story emerges in Daniel 1:6 and 17. Daniel was sturdy in his discipline because he had linked arms with others who shared his commitment. Daniel and his three buddies, Hananiah, Mishael, and Azariah, seemed to come as a package deal at least from the time of their captivity. This strong connection is seen throughout the book of Daniel. These young men knew that discipline is most easily maintained in a relationship with others who will stand with you.

7. When have you experienced the strength that comes from having others stand with you?

The Power of Sushi-sizing

The third thing that Daniel did to stay the course was that he sushi-sized his days (of course, that's a direct translation from the Hebrew manuscripts). This analogy probably only really works for you if you like sushi, but hang with me here. Discipline develops as we take one small bite of life at a time. The secret is that each small victory can lead to another and another, until the victories grow from sushi strips to whale flanks. And on top of that, each new discipline we take hold of can positively affect all the other disciplines we're trying to master. The smaller decisions of Daniel 1 set the young men on a course to stand against a fiery furnace in Daniel 3, a lion's den in Daniel 6, and the intense spiritual battles depicted in Daniel 7–12. None of us can swallow a whale or a tuna whole, but we can always pick up another piece of sushi.

session six

Read Matthew 6:34

8. How do we balance the message of this verse on not worrying about tomorrow with the concept of taking small steps of discipline today to prepare for the future?

The Power of Deep Dependence

Read Daniel 6:10

As we peek into Daniel's room, we get a view into what was probably Daniel's greatest secret in developing discipline and maintaining self-control. The vital ingredient for Daniel was a deep dependence upon the power of the Holy Spirit. He regularly—three times a day—gave thanks to God, and meditated on who He was and what He had done. He filled his mind with so much of God that there wasn't enough room for the enemy to mount a winning attack.

Meditation is mentioned over 52 times in Scripture. We aren't talking about the empty your head style of Eastern meditation. We are talking about biblical meditation, which has the power to completely transform your mind. In the best-selling book, Celebration of Discipline, Richard Foster instructs us in meditation. He writes, "Christian meditation is the ability to hear God's voice and obey His word. It's that simple. I wish I could make it more complicated for those who like things difficult." Meditation on God and His Word prepares the soil of our minds and hearts so that God can grow discipline (and other character qualities) in our lives.

So here's where discipline and meditation merge: Take out your calendar right now and schedule some times and locations for meditation over the next 30 days.

Read Zechariah 4:6 to discover the key to accomplishing anything.

9. What is the secret? Do you think Daniel knew it?

10. What might have occurred if Daniel had tried to fight the battles of his life in his own strength and power?

As a result of making right choices and developing godly discipline in his life, Daniel was head and shoulders above everyone else. Not only did Daniel's peers notice him, but the king also honored him and recognized the power of God because of Daniel's life.

Lift It Up

Daniel knew the secrets that create a life of discipline:
- Advanced planning
- Linking arms with others
- Sushi-sizing his days
- Daily meditation on God and His Word

11. Looking at the principles that Daniel embraced to go deep with discipline, which of these do you feel you need the most help with right now?

12. What specific area or aspect of your life would benefit the most right now from a fresh infusion of discipline or self-control?

Pray for each other that you will go deep with discipline. Ask God to give you small victories now in the areas where you struggle—victories that will lead you toward becoming a Daniel with renowned integrity and deep, lasting character.

My Prayer Needs:

_____
_____
_____
_____
_____
_____

My Group's Prayer Needs:

_____
_____
_____
_____
_____
_____
_____
_____
_____
_____
_____
_____

Leader's Guide

Whether you are a brand new small-group leader or a longtime veteran, this leader's guide is designed to help you make the most of your small-group time. It will help you facilitate a healthy discussion among the members of your group, as well as provide you with insight and answers to the questions in each session. Remember to check here not only for answers to questions you are not sure about, but also for ideas on how to involve everyone, how to bring creativity to the discussion, and how to delegate leadership to others.

Throughout this study there are a few places where you will encounter large sections of Scripture to be read. As the leader, you should encourage the members of your group to come to your meeting time prepared, having read the chapter, checked the Scripture references, and answered the questions. That way you can summarize these large blocks rather than risk losing people's attention while someone reads aloud. But, be careful not to assume that everyone knows these Bible stories, and make sure your summaries give the important points. Doing this will help you maintain a smooth flow in the discussion as you stay on target and on time in your small group.

Leading a small group can be a challenging experience, but it also brings many rewards, so invest some time in preparing yourself to lead. You will be delighted with the results!

Session One

Which Way Is Your Character Morphing?

1. What is one area of our society where you have seen moral standards slipping? Give an example.

   A: There will be a variety of answers to this question including politics, entertainment, marriages, education, youth attitudes, and others.

Leader's Guide

2. What are some practical ways to be a positive moral influence to the world around you?

> Tip: Make a short list of some of the suggestions or ideas people have. At the end of the discussion, share your list with the group members and challenge each person to go out and become a positive influence.

3. What are some ways you can stay connected to Jesus day in and day out?

> A: Answers might include prayer, reading the Bible, listening to Christian music, and more. A good follow-up question is, "How are you at doing that?"

4. Answers will vary.

5. What are the consequences of refusing to stay in the heat long enough to allow our impurities to rise to the top?

> A: God wants us to be a shining reflection of His glory, but we are tarnished by sin. When we say "no" to God's purification process, we stay mired in the muddy waters of a sinful life. The longer we stay in those muddy waters, the more corroded we become, and the farther from God we find ourselves.

6. Why do you think God uses suffering to reveal flaws and motivate character transformation?

> A: God uses suffering to show us our flaws and motivate us to change because it works! Tough times can make us more open to God's leadership as we realize that we don't have all the answers, and that we are dependent on Him. Suffering also has a way of clearing out the clutter so we can focus on what is really important in life.

7. What are the internal and external roadblocks that keep you from experiencing this transformation?

Leader's Guide

Tip: As the members of your group tell about their roadblocks, listen for similarities. Discuss ways to encourage one another in blasting through these barriers to become a clearer reflection of Christ.

8. When it comes to developing Christ-like character, what are the easy things we can do to help each other continue to grow? What are the hard things?

Tip: Use this question to lead into your time of prayer and praise. As a group, pray that God will open your eyes to opportunities to serve one another not only in the easy things, but also in the difficult areas of life.

Session Two

Will Your Endurance Hold Out?

1. Answers will vary.

2. Look back over your life and share an example where you wish you would have shown more endurance. What could have happened if you had seen the situation through?

Tip: A good follow-up question is, "Why do we so often give up on something before we get to the payoff?"

3. Answers will vary.

4. How do you imagine Noah "walked with God" on a daily basis? What might this "walk" look like today?

A: Noah's walk with God must have been very close for him to have been called "blameless among the people of his time." Surely it would have included regular prayer, ongoing worship, and the minute-to-minute decisions to follow God instead of his own impulses or the influence of the world around him.

Leader's Guide

5. Hebrews 11:1 says that "faith is being sure of what we hope for and certain of what we do not see." What do you think Noah's first reaction to God's request might have been? What kind of faith crises do you think he experienced before and during the construction process?

> Tip: An interesting follow-up question is, "In your own words, describe what it means to have faith."

6. Answers will vary.

7. What are some common reasons people give when they quit something?

> Tip: To keep the conversation going ask, "Are these legitimate reasons or just excuses?"

8. How can we determine when God wants us to endure in a situation and when He wants us to let something go?

> A: To keep our perspective on God's will, we need to review the teachings of Scripture regularly as the only reliable and absolute source about God's will for us. We also need to maintain our relationship with God through personal meditation and prayer, as well as corporate worship and prayer. God reveals and clarifies truth to us by His Spirit, who "searches all things, even the deep things of God" (See 1 Corinthians 2:10-16). But, be careful to "test the spirits to see whether they are from God" (1 John 4:1-3). It is also wise to consult other mature Christ-followers, including your pastor, church elders, and parents. Consult your circumstances and feelings last. They can also confirm God's direction for you.

9. Who in your life has a story that really gives you that extra boost you need to hang in there when endurance is required? Share the story.

> Tip: Be sure the group members explain what it is about this person that is an encouragement to others.

Leader's Guide

10. **What is one thing that you can throw off today that will help you run with more endurance?**

    A: There will be as many answers to this question as there are people in your group. After everyone who wants to has answered, ask what things the disciples gave up, or the Apostle Paul, or anyone else they know who is an example of endurance.

11. Answers will vary. Use this question to launch into your prayer time together.

Session Three

Is Your Courage Collapsible?

1. Answers will vary.

2. **What is the most courageous thing you have ever done? What did you have to overcome to follow through with action?**

    Tip: Use these two questions together by asking people to answer one or the other in your discussion time. Some of the stories may be long and some people may feel like they are "bragging" by telling a heroic story about themselves. Allowing people to choose a question will help alleviate both challenges.

3. **Given their incredible history with God, why do you think the Israelites were afraid now?**

    A: The Israelites' courage collapsed because they were looking at the task before them with a faulty focus. They were looking at what they could do, not what God could do through them. In addition, they, like we, are prone to forget what God has done for us in the past.

4. Maybe the grumblers had a point. After all it was THE

Leader's Guide

PROMISED LAND. Do you think they assumed that occupying it should be easier? Why do you think they felt that way?

> A: Sure, we all wish that God would just lay the blessings out for us to pick up, especially when we're ready to kick back and take a break from the struggles of life.

5. What "promised lands" have you had that were harder to occupy than you expected?

> Tip: A good follow-up question is, "How did you keep your courage up?"

6. Answers will vary.

7. Why is this approach to leadership so rare? What core human tendencies have to be overcome to act in this way?

> A: This type of leadership is rare because it requires a person to put aside pride. We have to publicly admit we are unable to control the situation and seek One who can. That goes against our natural tendency towards pride and self-sufficiency.

8. Does God's response seem fair and reasonable to you? Why didn't He just perform some great miracle right then to give them enough faith to go forward?

> A: God is the ultimate parent. He knew that if He just took care of this for the Israelites that they would become spoiled and lazy, just like children will if parents swoop in and get them "off the hook" when they disobey. He chose to allow them to experience consequences for their disobedience and doubt. There are still consequences for sin today, and God still works through them to draw us closer to Him.

9. Answers will vary.

10. Why does God repeat his command, "Be strong and courageous," so many times

Leader's Guide

A: He wanted to make sure His people got it! God knew that this had been a stumbling block before, so He encouraged Joshua. In turn Joshua's courage was contagious and the Israelites followed him across the Jordan into the promised land. God knows where we stumble, too, and He is encouraging us to be strong and courageous as we face our fears and follow Him.

11. What does the 40-year attitude makeover say about the nature of God's heart and His priorities?

A: This shows that God is just, but also that He is forgiving. God did not banish the Israelites to the desert forever or take away the land He had promised them. He disciplined them, but He also forgave them. Not only did God forgive Israel, but He also brought them back to the promised land and delivered it into their hands ... just as He had promised to do for their ancestors 40 years before. His priorities will always prevail, even when our sinfulness seems to get in the way.

12. Answers will vary. Use this question to launch into your prayer time together.

Session Four

Is God's Love Overflowing In You?

1. Answers will vary. Have fun with this question.

2. What was the first time you remember giving love to someone (or something) when it wasn't reciprocated?

Tip: A couple of good follow-up questions are, "Do you remember the first time you rejected someone else's love? How did that person respond?"

3. Why do you think God had Hosea marry an adulteress? How

Leader's Guide

does this fit with God's view of marriage in general?

A: God has always intended for marriage to be a picture of His loving relationship with us. Hosea was commanded to marry an adulteress as a symbol of the relationship Israel had created with God. He married her knowing she would be unfaithful some day, just as Israel was unfaithful to God. We are to be obedient to the guidelines God has given us for marriage today, just like Hosea was being obedient to God in his day.

4. Hosea pursued Gomer and she just kept running. When we run from God and refuse to turn back, what does He do? What have you seen him do in your life?

A: God never gives up on us. No matter how far or how hard we run, He is faithful in trying to bring us into a loving relationship with Him.

5. How do you imagine Gomer experienced the "thorns" as she was running away?

A: Answers will vary, but God kept her from her lovers by putting struggles in her life. These could have been illness, emotional anguish, a variety of difficult circumstances, and the like.

6. What is an example of how God has "barricaded you with thorny bushes" in your life?

Tip: As a follow-up question ask people how long they had to wander through the thorns and how much pain they had to endure before they turned back to God.

7. Why did Hosea quit providing for her? What do you think was His motivation?

A: Hosea quit providing for Gomer because she had turned away from him and into the arms of other men. His motivation was love. He loved her and wanted her to love him, so instead of providing for her so she could continue to live in rebellion,

Leader's Guide

he cut her provision off in hopes she would repent and return. Today we call this "tough love."

8. Answers will vary.

9. Answers will vary.

10. What are some things that you can do to help one another remain faithful to God or to help each other turn back to God in times of rebellion?

   Tip: Use this question to lead into your praise and prayer time. Ask God to help you stay faithful to Him as individuals and as a group.

11. Is it easy or difficult for you to accept God's amazing love? What does the Bible mean that "we love because he first loved us"?

   A: God is love (1 John 4:16) and we are made in His image (Genesis 1:27). Because of that, we can experience love and give love. Further, our love for others flows out of God's ongoing and unconditional love for us.

Session Five

Are You Riding the Crest of Creativity?

1. Answers will vary. Have fun with this question.

2. If you had unlimited funding and you knew you couldn't fail, what would you like to invent?

   Tip: It can be a lot of fun to have some play dough or modeling clay on hand and take a few minutes to make a model of your invention and tell about it. This kind of activity is great for getting people to relax and get involved.

Leader's Guide

3. Do you think we were all given the same amount of creativity? If not, why did God give more creativity to some than others?

> A: We are ALL creative, but by simply looking at the people around us it becomes obvious that we are all creative in different ways. God blesses each of us with different skill sets, talents, and gifts. For some, creativity is just a natural product of their design. For others, it comes out with effort and practice. We should all work to maximize our creative potential by putting our God-given creativity to work as often as possible!

4. Why do you think God has been so committed to creative communication techniques throughout history? Wouldn't it have been enough for Him to just thunder His voice from heaven?

> A: If we read the stories throughout the Bible, we see that there were many times when God communicated directly and people still didn't listen to Him. So, not hearing God's audible voice is really not the problem. Our refusal to listen is a heart problem.
>
> God chooses to communicate with us in creative ways because it is His nature and because it builds faith in us. When we take the time to really listen to Him, we are building a stronger relationship with Him—which is the point. As we see the effort He puts into reaching us, we see evidence of His love.

5. Answers will vary.

6. How can you apply Jesus' methods in the places you are called to be a spiritual influence?

> A: Jesus taught using common examples from the world around Him to illustrate His points. He used what was relevant to the time, place, and people where He was. All you have to do to follow Jesus' example of creativity is open your eyes to what is around you and think about how it relates to what you are trying to communicate. Then, consider the people around you so you will be aware of where they are coming from. This will enable you to meet them where they are.

Leader's Guide

7. What is it that blocks your creativity?

    A: Fear, laziness, lack of confidence, and poor preparation may be some of the most common answers. These blockers cause us all to get "creative cramps." The only cure for creative cramps is preparation. Some people think creativity and preparation cannot coexist, but creativity does not necessarily mean "spontaneity." Creativity is born from order, not chaos. Set up a plan that will help you overcome your "creative cramps."

8. In what area of your life (marriage, parenting, business, ministry, personal growth, etc.) do you feel the biggest need for increased creativity?

    Tip: Take note of the different areas where people want to become more creative. Look for opportunities in the weeks and months to come where you can encourage their creativity in those areas.

9. Answers will vary.

10. In which of these three areas do you struggle the most?
    Desire for more creativity
    Strategy for carrying out creativity
    Commitment to continuous creativity

    Tip: You can also ask in which area they feel they are strongest. As you enter the praise and prayer time of your group meeting, praise God for His creative genius and for the gift of creativity.

Session Six

Has Your Discipline Disintegrated?

1. What is the first thing you remember accomplishing as a young person that took a lot of discipline to complete?

Leader's Guide

Tip: Follow with, "How did it feel to stay the course and complete the project?"

2. In what areas of your life do you find it easiest to be disciplined? Which area is the hardest?

   Tip: This is a great place for you to model transparency. Take a little risk and share your personal discipline challenge. Tell why you struggle with that area and ask others why their discipline declines in their area of struggle.

3. How were these Israelites chosen for service in the king's court? What kind of pressure did this honored selection immediately create?

   A: They were chosen for their appearance and intellect. The pressure had to be high. They were identified as being a step above the rest in both their looks and brains. Now they had to live up to expectations. The king intentionally immersed these guys in his culture, attempting to win the best of the future leaders of Israel to his way of thinking.

4. Why was Daniel willing to risk so much in following his commitment not to eat the food that was defiled according to the laws of Moses?

   A: Daniel must have understood that accepting these foods was the first step in turning away from God and depending more on King Nebuchadnezzar. He wanted to be obedient in the "small things."

5. What are some things in our culture that threaten to take us away from the obedient, disciplined life God wants us to live?

   Tip: As people share their answers, write them down. Make copies of this list for the members of the group as a reminder about what is competing with God for our attention.

6. Answers will vary.

Leader's Guide

7. Answers will vary.

8. How do we balance the message of this verse on not worrying about tomorrow with the concept of taking small steps of discipline today to prepare for the future?

   A: The key word here is "worry." There is a difference in worrying about tomorrow and planning for it. Worriers let their emotions dictate their actions (or inaction), while planners let God guide them as they strategize how they will handle different situations that may arise in the future.

9. What is the secret? Do you think Daniel knew it?

   A: The secret is reliance on God, not our might, power, intelligence, or perseverance. Daniel is a great model for us today of how to depend on God no matter what comes our way.

10. What might have occurred if Daniel had tried to fight the battles in his life in his own strength and power?

    A: The Bible makes it clear that Satan is a formidable enemy and that the weapons of spiritual battle are spiritual. It seems likely that Daniel would have been steam-rolled at several points in his life without His dependence on God.

11. Looking at the principles that Daniel embraced to go deep with discipline, which of these do you feel you need the most help with right now?

    Tip: A good follow-up questions is simply, "Why?"

12. What specific area or aspect of your life would benefit the most right now from a fresh infusion of discipline or self-control?

    Tip: Use this question as a bridge to the praise and prayer time of your meeting.